Preaching Towards Church Revitalization and Renewal!

By
Tom Cheyney & Larry Wynn

Dedication (Tom)

To Cheryl, my beloved!

My best friend, life companion, and one who challenges me every day to be the best I can for my Lord. You mean the world to me. There are so many things I truly admire about you as a person, as my best friend and as my wife. Your smile lights up my soul. As a church revitalizer's wife, you have been courageous to go even when the path seemed unclear and yet the hand of God was certain. You have given much and sacrificed more so others might see Jesus. To all of those Church Revitalizers serving in local churches asking God to do great things once more and revive their church once more. The course is not easy, but the need is great and our Master longs to see the church restored for future generations.

"For God has not given us a spirit of fearfulness, but one of power, love, and sound judgment"
2 Timothy 1:7 HCSB

To God be the glory forever and ever.

Dedication (Larry)

There are so many people I owe a debt of gratitude to for living out these sermons. It is to these people I dedicate this book.

To my wife, who has been an encouragement for our 40 plus years of marriage. She has made the journey so much fun. She is a leader in her own rights who has been an example of the principles in this collection of sermons.

To our children, Amanda and Rando Acres, Dana Wynn, and Adam and Ivey Wynn. To our grandchildren Avery, Ryleigh, and Aligrace.

My family brings such joy to my life and inspires me greatly in the ministry with which God has entrusted me.

Acknowledgements

*T*om: I am blessed to serve each day the Greater Orlando Baptist Association (GOBA). This is a network of churches which is changing the way we have done associational work across Southern Baptist. No longer bound by geography, GOBA has raised the bar by working with churches, networks, and partners to plant healthy churches, to revitalize those churches in need of renewal, and to develop leaders equipped for the ministry through the GOAL Leadership Development Training. The Renovate National Church Revitalization Conference is one of these new things, which have impacted Christianity cross denominationally. Spearheaded by the wonderful pastors and laity who have partnered with us for the work of the Lord, may I say thank you.

To my many committed Church Revitalization Practioners who join with me annually to make the Renovate National Church Revitalization Conference the largest conference focused on helping declining churches, I thank you. Your gifts and your passion for hurting churches make my heart leap with such godly compassion. To those just beginning the journey seeks God's best and become the best daily so you become a vessel fully developed for the work of a church revitalizer.

Lastly to my Administrative Assistant, Linda Goans, who edited, and assured that these messages were comprehensible, thank you. Linda's commitment to growing from what had been done in the past to what is necessary for the future is to be rewarded. Her godly servant heart has been a blessing to me ever since I arrived to lead the effort as the Executive Director.

Larry: To the wonderful staff and members of Hebron Baptist Church. These are the people who embraced the principles found in this book. It was such a blessing to be their pastor for 33 years. I have never met a group of people with more vision and more commitment to reaching people with the message of Christ. There is no way I could name individuals. There are too many who impacted my life in incredible ways. Hebron Church will always hold a special place in my heart.

To my prayer partners with whom I met on a regular basis. They listened, offered counsel, and most importantly prayed with me for God's leadership in our church.

To two very special Denominational leaders Kevin Ezell and Dr. Robert White. These men have given me the opportunity to use my spiritual gifts to encourage and help equip pastors for the incredible ministry God has called them to.

To pastor friends, Ike Reighard and Frank Cox. These men fit every definition of a friend. They have walked with me through good times and difficult times. They have been a constant reminder of the value of friendship in the ministry.

Last but not least, my Administrative Assistant, Carol Ledbetter, who typed, retyped and made sure these sermons were understandable. Her commitment to living a missional lifestyle has been extremely valuable in communicating, in writing, the principles in this book.

What Others Are Saying
About *Preaching Towards Church Revitalization and Renewal!*

Knowing the ups and downs of church revitalization personally I can say that one of the most important platforms for pastors to communicate the concepts of renewal is the weekly message. Tom and Larry have captured the value of that event in this resourceful book! To have a library of teachable messages with revitalization at its heart gives pastors a huge head start on leading a church to rediscover Jesus' passion for the world. I am so grateful for Tom and Larry for being willing to step in with this book to help revitalizers teach their churches strategically towards renovation.

Jason Cooper,
Church Revitalizer and Pastor of The Church@Oaklevel

"Sometimes we just need to go back to the basics. Reading this book by my friend, Larry Wynn, reminded me of the simplicity of church growth and how we try to micro-manage the process. Larry Wynn and Tom Cheyney challenge us to reboot our efforts by re-examining the non-negotiable Biblical principles of growth. He also clearly illustrates them with 30 years of pastoral experience in the same church. I believe you'll find the Biblical Principles such as "letting your mission define your structure", "the priority of prayer", and "the constant need for a biblically clear focus" are communicated in ways that can be easily applied."

- Mike Landry, Senior Pastor,
Sarasota Baptist Church, Sarasota, Florida

Every week, every Pastor stands in a place that God has appointed for His message to His people to be proclaimed. The pulpit is where you lead alone with God and His authority. Sunday morning is yours as a Pastor; yours to lead your church to revitalization. This book will give you preaching resources that will help you put your church onto the right path. Dr. Cheyney and Dr. Wynn have complied great messages that will help you reignite your congregation.

Rob Myers, Pastor of Miami Baptist Church, Miami Florida
President of Baptist World Charities

I have the utmost respect for Tom Cheyney and Larry Wynn, and know their passion for the revitalization of Christ's Church well. Sometimes local church pastors are so overwhelmed by the revitalization needs that surround them, they do not know where to begin. In an effort to help these pastors to lovingly raise awareness and begin creating the needed urgency for revitalization change, Cheyney and Wynn have provided a series of model messages to gently bring the needed truth to bear.

I expect this book will be a very helpful tool in the hands of revitalization pastors everywhere – and especially those who find themselves in a revitalization work for the very first time. May God bless you with the wisdom, heart and endurance needed for the journey, knowing you are not alone!

Dr. John Kimball, CCCC Director of Church Development
Lead Planter/Pastor of Palmwood Church

"With 85 percent of churches plateaued or declining, church revitalization must be in the forefront of our discussion. Tom Cheyney and Larry Wynn are ones who understands the need and how to address all issues surrounding revitalization. They are practitioners who have a record in bringing an established and at that time, rural church back to life. In over 33 years of visionary leadership and obedience to God, he was used to build one of the great mega churches in the nation. Larry and Tom bring to this book, insight, vision and knowledge in revitalization

of a New Testament church. The knowledge they share is invaluable. Get ready to learn from some of the best."
- Frank Cox, Senior Pastor, North Metro Baptist Church,
Lawrenceville, Georgia

Solid, biblical preaching is the one thing that will renovate any and every church. Every time I have pastored a church that experienced a radical turn-around, I have found the preaching of God's Word to be my greatest resource.

Larry and Tom have a preacher's heart and their collection of sermons will equip you, the preacher, for the task of renovating. You will find that the Word preached on Sunday will be your greatest agent of change on Monday.

Ron Smith, author, Churches Gone Wild

While leading both church planting and church revitalization efforts, I found many more helpful resources for church planters than for leaders trying to turn a church around! This is especially true as it relates to messages designed to challenge and inspire churches in need of revitalization. Tom Cheyney and Larry Wynn have drawn from their passion and experience and given the church revitalizer a true gift in the pages of this book!
Lee Kricher, Pastor New Generation Church Pittsburg PA.

Though some may believe that the topic of Church revitalization is left largely unexplored in Scripture, the reality is that Scripture has a great deal to say on the topic. What is revitalization and renewal? What is necessary for revitalization and renewal? What are some examples of revitalization and renewal? All of these answers and more are found within the pages of Scripture. Tom Cheyney and Larry Wynn in their book, "Preaching Towards Church Revitalization and Renewal" outline the major threads of revitalization and renewal throughout Scripture for the church leader to reflect upon. This book will encourage leaders with the biblical passages, expectations, principles, and precepts necessary to carry out revitalization within their given ministry context. This book is a must have for all ministry and church leaders.

Michael Atherton, Lead Pastor Cornerstone Church
Lone Tree CO & Author of *The Revitalized Church*

"Over the past 25 years I have had the privilege to witness first-hand Larry Wynn lead an established church through the revitalization process to be a thriving, Great Commission church reaching many with the Gospel. As my pastor, I saw him lead with clarity and humility. As a mentor of mine for many years, I have been privileged to receive much help and insight as I have lead where God has placed me. What you will read isn't theory; it's wisdom that is proven to make a difference!"

Brian Stowe, Senior Pastor,
First Baptist Church, Plant City, Plant City, Florida

Casting the vision for revitalization and renewal requires a compelling presence in the pulpit. Congregations need to know that the vision for change is grounded in God's Word. Tom Cheyney and Larry Wynn have compiled sixteen sermons that provide pastors with the text and illustrations to begin a process of renewal and change that is both personal and congregational.

Rodney Harrison, Co-Author of SPIN-OFF Churches
and Pastoral Helmsmenship

"If I desire to read a "how to" book or a "help me" book, I want it to be written by a practitioner. That is exactly who Larry Wynn and Tom Cheyney are. They are leaders in their fields. Larry pastored one of the leading churches in America and he built it from scratch. Tom has led conferences and counseled many churches how to effectively revitalize a church. This is one book you do not want to tarry reading. Do it NOW!"

Jim Law, Executive Pastor,
First Baptist Church, Woodstock, Woodstock, Georgia

Revival and Church Revitalization both have absolute biblical verification. Tom and Larry are proclaiming the mandate for churches to walk in life, growth and revival by offering their experience and research. This book is a great tool to share with your congregation and comrades in the spiritual trenches. Grab one of the messages found inside, tweak it to fit your people and press them on toward godliness and growth!

Tracy Jaggers, Church Development Associate
Tryon Evergreen Baptist Association

The impressive combination of Tom Cheyney and Larry Wynn have teamed up to address one of the most critical areas of Church Revitalization, that of preaching for revitalization. Both men have been working in the area of church planting and church revitalization for many years and have something very important to say in an area nearly bereft of coverage. If pastors are going to address church revitalization, it should begin with their most effective medium – their public proclamation. Cheyney and Wynn have produced an invaluable resource for revitalization leaders.

Terry Rials, Church Revitalization Practioner
Oklahoma City, OK

I believe the most important prefix in the English language is RE. I am equally convinced that one of the most crucial issues facing Southern Baptist Churches today is that of Revitalization. Simply put, church revitalization is the process of becoming vital once again as a church in the community in which it exists. Larry Wynn and Tom Cheyney have co-authored this great book that will help with the challenges involved in creating a culture of revitalization. With more than 80% of Southern Baptist Churches, either plateaued or declining, it has become a life and death issue for many congregations. The good news is that "Preaching Towards Church Revitalization and Renewal" is a tool to help churches choose life by creating a game plan for revitalization.

I know from firsthand experience that revitalization can be accomplished because I pastor a church that is walking down this very path. I am pleased to say that Piedmont Church in Marietta, Georgia, is now averaging more people on Sunday mornings than ever before. This is occurring after the church was on the verge of closing its doors eight years ago. One of my favorite quotes that spurs me personally is: "The day your memories become greater than your dreams, you are dead in the water." Revitalization will give your congregation a new vision and dream that is so passion filled, that no one will talk about the "good old days", they will only ask, "What's Next?!"

- Dwight "Ike" Reighard, Senior Pastor,
Piedmont Church, Marietta, Georgia

Forward

The Seven Pillars of
Church Revitalization and Renewal

*O*ur Lord loves the local New Testament Church and it is His desire to see it grow! The need for Church Revitalization has never been greater in North America! An estimated 340,000 Protestant churches in America have an average attendance of less than one hundred.[1] Research data tells us that in the United States more than 80% of the churches have plateaued or are declining.[2] Each and every week we are currently seeing somewhere between fifty and seventy-five local churches closing their doors and not opening them again. Everything that must be done in the area of church revitalization cannot be accomplished in a few hours on the Lord's Day!

The most recent research data released in January of 2012 by the *Leavell Center for Evangelism and Church Health*, has said that within my own Southern Baptist Convention (SBC) we are at a critical juncture regarding church plateau and decline. The most recent series of studies have been conducted by Bill Day; Associate Director of the *Leavell Center for Evangelism and Church Health*, who serves the New Orleans Baptist Theological Seminary as the Gurney Professor of Evangelism and Church Health in his sequential

---

[1] Hartford Institute for Religious Research (hirr.hartsem.edu/research).

[2] Research Source: Stats listed online at: http://www.newchurchinitiatives.org/morechurches/index.htm (accessed 2/23/2006).

xvii

studies on church health and growth of 2003, 2007, and 2010. In January of 2012 Bill Day reported, that currently there are less than seven percent (6.8) of our SBC churches that are healthy growing churches. That means 3,087 of our 45,727 SBC churches are healthy. Even the number of SBC churches is in decline and we need to address the needs for church revitalization immediately.

<h3 style="text-align:center">Thinking About the Seven Pillars of
Church Revitalization</h3>

Working in the area of Church Revitalization will lead you eventually to consider the Seven Pillars of Church Revitalization. A Church Revitalizer will not be working in all of these areas at the same time, but you will eventually find yourself working in most of them at one time or another. Take a moment to reflect upon the Seven Pillars graph as we discuss these areas of renewal and revitalization.

Revitalization and Realignment

Perhaps the easiest pillar to address is revitalization and realignment. Some observers of church revitalization and renewal argue that the era of small churches is over and that the future belongs to the arising mega churches across North America. Granted mega is an amazing phenomenon of the past thirty years which seems to have arisen with the concept of the massive campus church. But to ignore the 340,000 plus churches in North America that average less than 100 weekly in church attendance would be ill advised! Those who serve and those who attend these churches are an enormously significant network of Christian influence. Even the mega church finds itself struggling to avoid plateau and decline.

A church in need of Revitalization is described as one where: there is the plateauing or declining after a phase of recent or initial expansion; then the church experiences the beginning of a high turn-over of lay leaders; there becomes a shorter duration of stay of fully assimilated people within the work; the church morale and momentum level drops; the church coasts for a brief time and then drops again, only to see the cycle of decline repeated again and again. The result is the church hits a new low! This new normal is the first sign of a church in need.

Refocusing

Refocusing is the second pillar and it helps churches that are growing, but still need to set new challenges and look for new opportunities to expand their gospel witness into their target area. Questions such as what is your biblical purpose and why do we exist as a congregation must be addressed. Looking at how God showed up in the past, is a good way to get the church unstuck by addressing where it has been, how God has worked, and what does He have for its future. Addressing the church's focus, vision, and leading them to discover God's new direction is just the beginning of helping a congregation to begin refocusing towards the Lord's new calling plan for the church! Many a pastor today has never been taught how to grow a church and they feel quite stuck and in need of someone to come along side of them and challenge them to refocus one's self and the church!

Re-visioning

A little bit harder certainly, but not as hard, as the descending order of decline that will eventually lead to the *Restarting* pillar of revitalization. Have you ever seen a church that once was alive and vital begin to lose its focus and drive for the cause of Christ? That is a church that needs to work on its Re-visioning strategy! Any *Re-visioning* strategy works to help churches dream new dreams and accomplish new goals that lead towards re-growing a healthy church! This strategy is designed for a weekend retreat tailored fit to foster a sense of ownership and team ship related to discovering a shared vision for the church.

Understanding the critical milestones necessary for a new vision will help foster healthy church practices that might have been lost. Something as simple as achieving a great goal of some sort can begin to launch a church back into a *Re-visioning* strategy. Something as simple and dangerous as the Lord's children taking an ill advised rest that resulted in a slowing or stalling of the momentum into a maintenance mentality can cause a church to become stuck.

Renewing

Church Renewal is the forth pillar of the seven pillars of Church Revitalization process. Often the church simply needs to get back to that which was working and get back on track. When that is needed, a careful renewal strategy needs to be planned and carried out. Renewing a congregation becomes much harder than the refocusing, re-visioning and revitalization process. Not everyone who works in church renewal is wired the exact same way and it is important to understand each congregation's individual needs and not try to make a one size fits all! There is no magic pill in church revitalization. Far too much writing on church growth of the 1980's was designed in a one size fits all "bigger is better" model and while it may not have been the only cause for declining numbers in our churches, but it certainly contributed! It is vital that you prepare the laity for the work of church renewal as well as yourself. Communicate early and often with the church how the renewal process will take place and how it will be implemented. Prepare yourself spiritually and then prepare your leaders spiritually. Then begin preparing your church spiritually for renewal! A *Church Renewal Weekend* is a great way to start! Church renewal is not about finding the magic medication or treatment to get growing. It is more about discovering God's vision for the church and practicing it for the long haul. The utilization of a Church Renewal weekend works well to draw God's people back towards health and vitality.

Reinvention

This fifth pillar of Church Revitalization deals with tools and techniques to assist the church when it is necessary to reinvent itself to a changing community. When a church experiences a shift in the community makeup, often there will be to various degrees, the need to redevelop a new experience for those who make up the new church context! New experiences must replace old experiences. New practices likewise will replace old practices. A church that is experiencing the need for reinvention must take seriously the need and make the commitment for reinventing itself, revaluing itself, reforming itself, and reinvigorating itself to fit the new context.

Restoration

This sixth area of Church Revitalization deals with things a church and a minister must go through when circumstances necessitate that a restoration process is called for! Things such as:

Gaining a new and fresh understanding of the new future for the church is vital if success is in the church's future.

Inspiring new prospects with a vision that is both compelling and motivational. Prospects seek to be inspired and not dragged down in the world in which we live in.

Meet new needs in order to give you a restored place among the community in which you seek to further minister.

Become prospect driven during these days of transition. Look for new and yet to be reached opportunities to minister.

Remember if you try to do everything you will end up doing nothing. Therefore pick your greatest opportunities first and let the rest follow along later.

Craft something that comes out of a community in flux and look for ways to reconnect to the community where you once were firmly entrenched. Keep in mind you have been given a second chance so don't blow it. Prayerfully seek the new things because it might be something you will be doing for a long, long time!

Restarting

The final Pillar of Church Revitalization is the hardest and often only happens once the church's patriarchs and matriarchs have tried everything else they could think of to grow the church with no success! The challenge here is that most churches wait too long to enter into this area of revitalization and by the time they are willing to utilize this strategy, they have sucked out all of the life within the church and it is no longer a viable candidate for this effort. When a sick church no longer has the courage to work through the various issues that led to its poor health, it is usually identified as being on life support and in need of a restart. This type of church has been flat-lined and just holding on by means of its legacy and the faithful few who attend. The Restarting Strategy (also known as a Repotting strategy) is for an unhealthy church to once again begin growing and to engage in a renewed vision that is demonstrated through sufficient evidences of hope. The restart based church revitalization model is being used all across North America. Any group planting churches or working in the area of Church Revitalization should have a restart strategy if it is going to be a wise steward. One critical point from the start is a complete change of leadership and direction. This is a must for this revitalization model to be successful. Lyle Schaller reminds us that 85,000 evangelical churches are running fewer than 50 on Sunday. Being aware of their "critical" condition, however, is not enough. They have got to become convinced they need "major" surgical treatment. One church I have worked with still believes that they have more to offer, though their decline has been meteoritic and yet, they refuse to allow a restart to take place.

Changing the mindset of the residual membership can often be very difficult. Senior adults occupy most of these restart candidate churches for which change is often hard to come by. Until the church is ready to make drastic changes, it is useless to become involved. There are thousands of churches like this all over America: Some are Baptists, others are Methodists, even in the Assemblies you can find them, Presbyterians, the Lutherans have them, Congregational, Christian, and many others, waiting for a mission-minded congregation to get involved in offering "new life."

One startling phenomena is there are churches today that as the laity begin to depart this life often see nothing wrong with taking the church to the grave as well. That was never part of God's plan for the very thing He gave up His life.

Table of Contents

Introduction

Putting Cranberries and Nuts in the Bread

————— ✸ —————

$\mathcal{W}$hat does the introduction title of putting cranberries and nuts into your bread have to do with the subject of preaching towards church revitalization and renewal? It is fascinating that churches that are being revitalized are often wonderful examples of adding cranberries or nuts to the mixture. *Preaching Towards Church Revitalization and Renewal* is a book of sermons about grabbing the hearts of those recipients of the gospel message in a way to provide the best opportunity to lead the church towards revitalization. Adding a little spice and a little protein is always helpful to any mixture.

> My wife, Cheryl makes wonderful Cranberry Nut Bread each Thanksgiving for our family and friends to enjoy. The bread mix is pretty basic, but once she adds the cranberries, orange juice, and the walnuts, a plain recipe becomes something incredible.

Pastors which are stuck in the decline of their church, are often preaching just to get another week out of the way. There is little expectation from their preaching both from themselves as the preacher and from the remaining participants attending the local church. Visitors come and go quickly, because they find nothing fresh or full of flavor for them to remain. While in college, I heard a professor share an Arab proverb, which has stuck with me. Although I cannot recall the author or even which class I was taking at the time, the proverb has remained with me for more than forty plus years. The proverb is simple: *The best speaker is one who turns ears into eyes.*

Proclamation of the revitalization message must take the listeners from habitual listeners to responsive visualizers of the message and need for renewal. Preaching with the goal of helping a church begin the journey of revitalization and renewal is different than standing up each Lord's Day and simply preaching a gospel centered message. First, if you are going to lead your church into a church revitalization effort you must be willing to invest a minimum of one thousand days into the effort. Most pastors practice in preaching one series after another with perhaps only a week or two in between where a great theme of the Bible might be preached. But preaching towards church revitalization and renewal is different. There are certainly many passages throughout both the Old and New Testaments, which speak to revitalization and restoration. But if you are going to preach in an attempt to prepare your people for the next three-year effort, than having the ability to layer your preaching towards the end goals will be necessary. God restores His churches through the bringing of the participants to individual repentance, communal faith, and corporate obedience. If the Lord has called you to preach towards church revitalization and renewal, then you will need to reflect upon everything you are, what you are, and how God might use you in His plan for renewal of the church your serve.

If you are to enjoy the next three years of leading your people towards a church turnaround, you must become busy in the work of revitalization and leave out the many things which are probably distracting you from the goal. If you believe that your weekly preaching is the primary thing you are called to do, it is then vital that you make every effort towards focusing that effort toward the renewal of you, your people and your congregation. While no two preachers can preach the same message, these sermons serve as a launching pad for your study and sermon preparation as it relates to church revitalization and renewal. Great preaching is relevant to the listeners and those listeners of a declining church need for you to focus on re-strengthening the work of the local church. While all of us would profit from this work on church revitalization and renewal, there are two types of revitalization preachers that most need this work. The first one is the brand new unproven Church Revitalizer just called to a church in need of revitalization. Learn as much as you can about church revitalization as you seek to learn yourself into the future. Become a student of church revitalization and attend the Renovate National Church Revitalization Conference annually to grow and to rub shoulders with the leaders and national voices of this movement. The second type of pastor which really needs this work is the experienced pastor of three to five churches which has never been able to turn one around and has gone from one church to another hoping to be a success in the next placement. These are the ones which are perhaps the most in need of a little encouragement through this work.

Preaching Towards Church Revitalization and Renewal is a book that holds preaching as a critical key to every church's revitalization efforts. Proclamation from the pulpit by God's pulpiteer is fundamental to every renewal effort. Preaching towards revitalization is the initial step for a church desiring to turnaround. Preaching focused on revitalization can become the beginning phase of eliminating the continual drift that is taking place in so many churches. Preachers revitalize churches. Declining churches need preachers to strongly proclaim the need for renewal. Without a biblical challenge towards renewal there is no revitalization. What I have seen over and over again in working with churches, which are being revitalized through the blessings of God, is that as the preacher becomes renewed, the pulpit becomes renewed and it is the beginning of the journey towards revitalization.

The Reality of the Need for Revitalization in North America

The hard reality in North America is that most churches and most, if not all, denominations are in a state of decline. The membership within these churches and denominations is plateauing and what used to pass for involvement and activity within churches is deteriorating. While all of this is happening, the rank and file of the church appears powerless to assemble the strength that is needed to get the churches growing again. In 1990, an editor for the Wall Street Journal Wade Clark Roof published an editorial article entitled, *"The Episcopalian Goes the Way of the Dodo,"* where he argued the decline of mainline denominationalism and its effect on Christianity.[3] With the turn of the twenty-first century sustained growth within our churches is an intermittent exception while decline seems to be more of the pronouncement. The mainline denominations, to which Roof referred, are still in the midst of severe decline and serious deterioration.

If the estimates are accurate that, at a minimum eighty percent or more of our churches are in need of revitalization, then it stands to reason that the majority of graduates from our seminaries are going to begin their ministries in the majority of these churches. Less than five percent of these graduates will actually be going to healthy churches. Existing ministers will pastor the healthy pool of churches that make up the twenty percent so the seminarian needs to prepare for the eventual challenge of revitalizing a plateaued or declining church. While we must start with reencountering the divine and realizing any church which is revitalized or becoming revitalized is the work of our Lord God, we must do our part to provide tools and methodologies for today's ministers to assist them with new practices and approaches that can help today's declining churches. Our Southern Baptist churches must not remain in stained glass, red bricked, spiral castles giving out apologies for lack of renewal or mixed gestures towards revitalization efforts.

Fast Facts for Future Church Revitalizers

There are:

- 340,000 churches are in need of church revitalization today.
- Ninety-five percent (95 percent) of churches in North America average 100 or less.
- Over eighty percent (80 percent) of American Churches are in decline or on a plateau.

---

[3] Wade Clark Roof, *"The Episcopalian Goes the Way of the Dodo,"* Wall Street Journal, July 20, 1990.

- Each year approximately 3,500 churches die in North America.
- Within my own Southern Baptist Convention, the annual death rate averages between seven and nine hundred!
- Studies have shown that churches typically plateau in attendance by their fifteenth year, and by year 35 they begin having trouble replacing the members they lose.
- Only 7.3 % of small churches are growing in North America currently.
- Of the churches, which are fifty years old or older, only 9.2% are growing.
- In North America, fifty to sixty churches close their doors every week.
- Among churches of all sizes, growing churches are rare! In fact, they only make up about 20 percent of our churches today.
- The other 80 percent have reached a plateau or are declining.
- The average church attracts fewer than 90 adults on a typical weekend.
- 60 % of protestant churches have 100 or fewer adults on a typical weekend.

In the Old Testament the prophets gave full attention to preaching God's Word. Jesus Christ in the New Testament continues that refrain. The Apostles which came after continued the preeminence of the Word of God in preaching. It goes without saying that what a preacher places as the most important thing within his ministry, will become the chief priority of the congregation he leads. If he keeps the preaching towards church revitalization and renewal the main thing, the church has a greater chance in accomplishing the turnaround of the declining ministry. Every Lord's Day, I look forward to being able to preach the Word of God for it is not something I dread. Rather it is something I blessed by being called to do and that is exciting to me and I work at conveying this excitement to the people who hear me preach. When the pulpit lacks excitement and become monotonous, there will be a loss of passion to point the way for those who need it most. *Preaching Towards Church Revitalization and Renewal* could become a source for three or four sermon series targeted at the introduction of a journey and challenge for change bringing about renewal. Revitalization preaching has the air of assessment, anticipation, and adventure. It assesses where a church is with the real facts and figures while showing that as the leader you are willing to lead them through the process. It paints a picture of anticipation of what could be if we confess our sins individually and corporately. It brushes the congregation with a view of the journey before us, which reminds all of us of the adventure.

I want to thank my dear friend, Larry Wynn for having the heart to join me in sharing with you some proven messages intended to be preached in various sermon series to help a local church begin raising the issue of revitalization and renewal. There are many "how-to-preach" books out there but this is the only one focused on preaching towards revitalization and renewal by providing you with messages we have both preached at churches all over North America. Keep watching for more in this series by checking out the bookstore at: RenovateConference.org or by attending the annual national conference each year. We welcome you to attend the first week of November in Orlando.

For the cause of church revitalization and renewal,

Tom Cheyney and Larry Wynn
2 Timothy 1:7

Chapter 1

Battered Bones and Busy People:

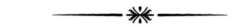

Things we need in order to have revitalization in our churches!
Ezekiel 37:1-14

The hand of the LORD was on me, and He brought me out by His Spirit and set me down in the middle of the valley; it was full of bones. He led me all around them. There were a great many of them on the surface of the valley, and they were very dry. Then He said to me, "Son of man, can these bones live?" I replied, "Lord GOD, only You know." He said to me, "Prophesy concerning these bones and say to them: Dry bones, hear the word of the LORD! This is what the Lord GOD says to these bones: I will cause breath to enter you, and you will live. I will put tendons on you, make flesh grow on you, and cover you with skin. I will put breath in you so that you come to life. Then you will know that I am [4]Yahweh." So I prophesied as I had been commanded. While I was prophesying, there was a noise, a rattling sound, and the bones came together, bone to bone. As I looked, tendons appeared on them, flesh grew, and skin covered them, but there was no breath in them. He said to me, "Prophesy to the breath, prophesy, son of man. Say to it: This is what the Lord GOD says: Breath, come from the four winds and breathe into these slain so that they may live!" So I prophesied as He commanded me; the breath entered them, and they came

---

[4] C.f. Joel 2:27; 3:17.

*to life and stood on their feet, a vast army. Then He said to me, "Son of man, these bones are the whole house of Israel. Look how they say, 'Our bones are dried up, and our hope has perished; we are cut off.'Therefore, prophesy and say to them: This is what the Lord G*OD *says: I am going to open your graves and bring you up from them, My people, and lead you into the land of Israel. You will know that I am Yahweh, My people, when I open your graves and bring you up from them. I will put My Spirit in you, and you will live, and I will settle you in your own land. Then you will know that I am Yahweh. I have spoken, and I will do it." This is the declaration of the L*ORD*.* [5]

God's people desperately need a biblical base for church revitalization! Many Christians today actually attend a local church, which needs to consider learning and practicing the various principles for Revitalizing Churches. In 1990 an editor for the Wall Street Journal Wade Clark Roof published an editorial article entitled, "The Episcopalian Goes the Way of the Dodo," where he argued the decline of mainline denominationalism and its effect on Christianity.[6]

Some *Quick Facts* regarding Church Revitalization and Renewal:

- There are 344,000 protestant evangelical churches from the eight mainline denominations in the western hemisphere, which are in plateau and decline.
- 95% of churches in North America average 100 or less.
- Over 82% of American Churches are in decline or on a plateau.
- Each year 3,500 to 4,000 churches die in North America (900 last year within my Denomination alone).
- Within my own Southern Baptist Convention the annual death rate averages between seven and nine hundred.

---

[5] *The Holy Bible: Holman Christian Standard Version.* (Nashville: Holman Bible Publishers, 2009), Ezekiel 37:1–14.

[6] Wade Clark Roof, "The Episcopalian Goes the Way of the Dodo," Wall Street Journal, July 20, 1990.

- Studies have shown that churches typically plateau in attendance by their fifteenth year, and by year 35 they begin having trouble replacing the members they lose.
- Only 7.3 % of small churches are growing in North America currently.
- They have the inability to regain the critical mass necessary to regrow the church utilizing the tools and techniques they are presently employing.
- 50 – 60 churches in North America close their door every week.
- Of the churches, which are fifty years old or older, only 9.2% are growing.
- Among churches of all sizes, growing churches are rare! In fact, they only make up about 20 percent of our churches today.
- In a study of more than two thousand churches, David Olson revealed that 69 percent of our churches in America have reached a plateau or even worse are declining.
- Jim Tomberlin and Warren Bird declare that "80 percent of the three hundred thousand Protestant churches in the United States have plateaued or are declining, and many of them are in desperate need of a vibrant ministry."
- A more recent series of studies (The State of the Church) was conducted by Bill Day; Associate Director of the Leavell Center for Evangelism and Church Health, who serves the New Orleans Baptist Theological Seminary as the Gurney Professor of Evangelism and Church Health in his sequential studies on church health and growth of 2003, 2007, and 2010. where he reports that currently there are less than seven percent (6.8) of our SBC churches which are healthy growing churches. That means 3,087 of our 45,727 SBC churches are healthy.
- About 63 million people of the population attend church each Sunday (American Sociological Review).
- The average church attracts fewer than 90 adults on a typical weekend.
- 60 % of protestant churches have 100 or fewer adults on a typical weekend

- Just 2% of churches attracts more than 1,000 adults on a typical weekend.
- In the United States protestant churches there are 9 million weekly worshipers in attendance.
- There are 177,000 churches with less than 100 people. That is 59% of all churches in the United States (National Congregation Study).
- 90% of congregations have 350 or fewer people.
- One interesting note is that churches of 200 or less, they are four times more likely to plant a church than churches of 1,000 or more.
- The smaller the church the more fertile they are in planting churches (LifeWay).

The hard reality is this:

"It can be said that most churches in almost any North American denomination is in rapid decline or plateauing in its membership! Involvement within these churches is dwindling and the laity seems powerless to muster the strength needed to get it growing again."[7]

Church Revitalization is important because so many churches are dying and or are all but dead. It is also important because even today's healthy churches run the risk of developing the same illness that other churches are experiencing.

Let us consider the church revitalization theme *"Battered Bones and Busy People: Things we need in order to have revitalization in our churches!"*

In the town of Sedlec in the Czech Republic there is a famous cemetery that dates back to the 13th century. Some 40,000 people who died from the Black Plague in the 14th century and in the Hussite wars in the beginning of the 15th century were buried there. Around 1400 a Gothic church of *All Saints* was built at the center of the cemetery. Underneath it a chapel was built as an ossuary to hold the bones unearthed in mass graves during the construction of the church. This

---

[7] Adapted from: *Boomerang Churches: How a Church Returns to its Calling,* By Tom Cheyney.

church of bones contains the skeletal remains of these 40,000 people. It is literally a church of bones.[8]

As I travel all across this country some churches still have cemeteries on their properties. Yet, your church does not have to have a cemetery to have broken bones and dead bodies all around. Listen, if we do not keep evangelism as a top priority in our church revitalization efforts, we will even have some pews occupied by individuals with dead spirits. If we are honest sometimes the whole assembly of people can feel dead.

Look with me at a congregation of *Battered Bones and Busy People*:

> *"The hand of the LORD was upon me, and he brought me out by the Spirit of the LORD and set me in the middle of a valley; it was full of bones"* Ezekiel 37:1 NIV.

Now Ezekiel was not in California, but it could have been called Death Valley. What he saw was not flesh and bones, but bones. He saw the dried bones of formerly busy people who had other things to do besides walking close to God! You know the story: The Hebrew people were living as exiles in Babylon. Nebuchadnezzar and the Babylonian army had destroyed Jerusalem and forced the people to live in Babylon. They were far from their home, they were lost, and dried up, wondering if their identity as a nation was nothing but a corpse. They were remindful that a couple of hundred years before, their fellow Hebrews, who had lived north of them, were defeated by the Assyrians, taken into exile, and never heard from again.

Churches today as well as individual believers today can begin to acknowledge the truth that life can get dry. Often our busyness in a thousand other things, besides the ministry and work of the local church and association, can cause us to feel fragmented and shattered. When churches become dry and believers become dry towards the Lord, it is so discouraging! Discouragement is one of Satan's extreme tools for destroying churches and individuals. I want to tell you that

---

[8] **http://sedlecossuary.com/Sedlec-Ossuary-Facts.html** (accessed 10/5/2014).

the single greatest weapon that the devil has to use against the people of God is discouragement. If the devil can get you discouraged then you will not pray. If the devil can get you discouraged then you will not read the Bible. If the devil can get you discouraged then you will not come to church. If the devil can get you discouraged then you will quit looking to Jesus. What we are left with is busy people and broken bones, which are dry.

Because of this weapon of discouragement, statistics tell us:

1,500 pastors leave the ministry permanently each month in America.

80% of pastors and 85% of their spouses feel discouraged in their roles.

70% of pastors do not have a close friend, confidant, or mentor.

Over 50% of pastors are so discouraged they would leave the ministry if they could but have no other way of making a living.

Over 50% of pastors' wives feel that their husband entering ministry was the most destructive thing to ever happen to their families.

30% of pastors said they had either been in an ongoing affair or had a one-time sexual encounter with a parishioner.

71% of pastors stated they were burned out, and they battle depression beyond fatigue on a weekly and even a daily basis.

One out of every ten ministers will actually retire as a minister.[9]

Because of this weapon called discouragement the people of God become down hearted, hopeless, burdened and weary in well doing and become a valley of dry bones.

---

[9] C.f. Witt, Lance. *Replenish: Leading from a Healthy Soul*, (Grand Rapids: Baker Books, 2011).

The potential for a church to get bone dry should always concern us. Bone yards are graveyards. In some respects churchyards would make great cemeteries. We might be organized, uniform, perfect in appearance, yet there is no transformation, no willingness to change for the good of the community, and no courage to stop listening to the complainer and start running with the runners! Ezekiel declares in verses 2 & 3:

"He led me back and forth among them, and I saw a great many bones on the floor of the valley, bones that were very dry. He asked me, "Son of man, can these bones live?"

Now dry bones are as dead as you can get! The prophet walked "back and forth" (lit. "around") in the valley taking care not to touch any of the bones. The bones were characterized as "very dry," indicating that they had been there for some time (Ezekiel 37:2).[10] Any proposition that there could ever again be life in the bones would appear ridiculous. Yet as Ezekiel surveyed the scene in the valley of bones, he heard a question, *"Son of man, can these bones live?"* (v. 3). He knew that if the bones could be brought back to life, it was a matter only God understood and that the giving of that life once more was a deed only God could accomplish. These bones are not still moist with decaying flesh but the emphasis is that the bones were *VERY DRY*. It is one thing to believe God for a miracle to heal the sick or maybe even to raise a person who has died recently like Lazarus. You would think the answer had to be "NO". But Ezekiel hesitates and declares:

"O Sovereign LORD, you alone know"
Ezekiel 37:3b NIV.

Here is the question for all of us as we have gathered together: *Can you revitalize your church and bring back life into your church*

---

[10] Lamar Eugene Cooper, *Ezekiel*, vol. 17, The New American Commentary (Nashville: Broadman & Holman Publishers, 1994), 323.

if you are spiritually dry, emotionally discouraged and physically dead? We are going to share about things we need in order to get vitality back into our churches and into each one of us.

1. **The Presentation of the Vision: We need to GET A FRESH WORD FROM THE LORD**

> *Then He said to me, "Prophesy to these bones and say to them, 'Dry bones, hear the word of the LORD!*
> Ezekiel 37:4 NIV

Can you imagine a more difficult assignment: Preach to a bunch of bones? Now that is a tough congregation! I know the name of that church and so do you. It is known as Bone Yard Baptist Church.

Is it not interesting that these "Dry bones" did not get a dry sermon? What they got was a divine word from the Lord! They did not receive a word from an economist, nor Dr. Phil, nor Rush, not a personal ad, but they received a divine word from the Lord.

Ezekiel was called to be God's mouthpiece, not delivering Ezekiel's message but the Lord's. Each of us who are preachers of the Gospel, have that same calling. If ANYONE can speak to dry inanimate objects and have them respond, it is the Lord our God.

Now notice that:

He spoke to wind–peace be still.
He spoke to the waves–part so my people may pass
He spoke to the rocks and they brought forth water.
He spoke and they heard and responded.

Should it not also be true that the bones would hear? The word of the Lord is a word of life. As the hymn writer stated: *Sing them over and over again, wonderful words of life*. The power of this vision has brought hope to many down the span of time. The power of God can change even the most hopeless of lives and situations.

Listen church: Whatever it is that you face, whatever your circumstances, God has something to say. Can these bones live? We need to GET A FRESH WORD FROM THE LORD. Yet more is needed.

2. The Construction of the Vision: We need to GET TOGETHER as a church

> *So I prophesied as I was commanded. And as I was prophesying, there was a noise; a rattling sound, and the bones came together, bone to bone. I looked, and tendons and flesh appeared on them and skin covered them, but there was no breath in them* (Ezekiel 37:7-8 NIV).

Now notice they begin to click together making a rattling sound like Legos coming together. The scripture announces: They got together! The foot bone was connected to the anklebone. The anklebone was connected to the shinbone. The shinbone connected to the knee bone and on it went!

They come together into a complete skeleton. Some people are the backbone of God's church through supporting ministries. Some people are the leg bones of God's church, capable of doing the heavy lifting, while moving the church forward. Some people are the hands of God's church with the ability to touch others. Some people are the jawbone of God's church able to speak the Word of the Lord. Some people are the Kneebone of God's church able to bow in prayer. Some have a keen ability to listen to people who need a friend.

Now God has no room in church revitalization for mere wishbones. These are the folks who wish things were different, but are not willing to work to bring about change. God has no knucklebones in church revitalization. You see these people everywhere. They are willing to fight everybody and every thing in order to get their way.

Chuck Colson said that when people asked what church he attended, he said he did not just attend a church, he BELONGED to one. Then he named his church. You do not just attend a church; you belong to the church. Can these bones live? We need to GET A FRESH WORD FROM THE LORD. We need to GET TOGETHER.

3. The Elevation of the Vision: We need to rise up and GET GOD'S SPIRIT

Then he said to me, "Prophesy to the breath; prophesy, son of man, and say to it, 'This is what the Sovereign LORD says: Come from the four winds, O breath, and breathe into these slain, that they may live'" Ezekiel 37:9 NIV.

I will put my Spirit in you and you will live Ezekiel 37:14a NIV.

Notice that these bones find their very life in the acts of a God who can actually revive the dead. The local church stuck in rapid decline may also find its very renewal in the acts of God. Ask anyone else can these bones live? And the answer is clear. NO WAY! Yet God is able. Jesus is willing and the Holy Spirit is anxious for any church to seek Him again. The Lord God assured these discouraged captives of Israel, that he would resurrect his people from this death-like captivity. While the people of Israel felt that their hope was dead in Babylon, God was able to say, *"You will live."* He would open their graves and then cause his people to come out of their graves as God was able to say, *"You will live."* Then the Lord would bring them back to their land as God was able to say, *"You will live."* This miraculous transformation would be accomplished through the Holy Spirit of God, which God would put within his people as God was able to say, *"You will live."*

When Jesus Christ was rejected and reviled, flogged and finally killed on a cruel cross, God was able to say, *"You will live."* When the early church faced opposition and persecution of such intensity the desire was to make Christianity extinct, God was able to say, *"You will live."* When we were *"dead in our trespasses and sins,"* God was able to say, *"You will live."* When we are crushed by guilt, without vision, overwhelmed, under attack, stuck in a barren place, at the end of our rope, when we have no place to go, when we are without hope, God is able to say, *"You will live."* Regardless, if you are spiritually dry, mentally discouraged, or physically disconnected from God, we can still hear God say, *"I will put my spirit within you, and you shall live."*

As Rick Warren says in the *The Purpose-Driven Church*, "You will never know that God is all you need until God is all you've got."[11] This passage within Ezekiel challenges us to open ourselves to the life-giving power of God's Spirit. Church Revitalization and Renewal is the Lord's way to give life to declining churches. As you read this passage may you begin to read it through the eyes and ears of the prophet Ezekiel.

God is saying to you right now and in the days to come: Be my mouthpiece for Church Revitalization and Renewal. Deliver my message for Church Revitalization and Renewal. Go to those churches, which are dry and lifeless and let them know that there is hope. May I ask each and every one of us this evening hearing this message some questions: Is there dryness deep down in your bones? Is there a dryness that will not go away? Is there a thirst, which cannot be quenched? The valley of dry bones speaks of the spiritual condition of the nation. And if we are to learn anything from this, we have to see that it also speaks of our nation.

God caused the prophet to pass back and forth among bones— and we do this every day in the shops and on the streets of our towns and cities. What do we see? Do we feel the situation of our communities? Jesus did, and he wept over Jerusalem. Paul did, and his heart's desire and prayer for his nation was that they should be saved.

It may be that we feel totally inadequate to meet the needs of today, but we could not be more inadequate than Ezekiel in the valley of dry bones. Our adequacy is no more the issue than the condition of the bones. What really matters is this: do we trust God to work?

God did not send a social reformer to this valley, neither did he send a politician or an educator; rather, he sent a preacher! Ezekiel was in that valley, not at the invitation of the dry bones and not by his own inclination, but he was there by the sovereign will of God. God promises nothing about the future except that it will be God's and ours together and that life can come out of dry bones.

---

[11] C.f. Warren, Rick. *The Purpose-Driven Church*, (Grand Rapids: Zondervan, 1995).

The God who brought Ezekiel from despair to hope, who brought hope to a defeated nation and who raised Jesus from the dead is our God. This God is more powerful than all the sin of humankind and all the forces of destruction at work in the universe. May this God breathe life into our nation and world. May this God be with us, keep us close and breathe life into us. We need not be afraid, though we walk through the valley of the shadow of death or find ourselves in a valley of dry bones.

We need to: We need to GET A FRESH WORD FROM THE LORD. We need to GET TOGETHER as a church and as an association! We need to let GOD'S SPIRIT do what it alone can do.

Chapter 2

A Church Model for all Generations

Acts 2:42-47

"And they continued steadfastly in the apostles' doctrine and fellowship, in the breaking of bread, and in prayers. Then fear came upon every soul, and many wonders and signs were done through the apostles. Now all who believed were together, and had all things in common, and sold their possessions and goods, and divided them among all, as anyone had need. So continuing daily with one accord in the temple, and breaking bread from house to house, they ate their food with gladness and simplicity of heart, praising God and having favor with all the people. And the Lord added to the church daily those who were being saved." (Acts 2:42-47 NKJV)[12]

There are many models for doing church today. Churches come in all shapes and sizes. There are a multitude of worship styles, structures, and approaches to ministry represented in today's church. People are constantly asking, "What is the best approach?" The truth is there is not a "one size fits all" approach that is effective in every church. Practices that will work in one situation may or may not work in another situation or location.

---

[12] Scripture quotations are taken from the New King James Version (Nashville, TN: Thomas Nelson, Inc., Publishers, 1979, 1980, 1982).

There are principles that will be effective across generational, cultural, and geographical lines. Churches that are reaching people and are impacting their communities for Christ have some things in common. These are the principles I am talking about. They are found in the book of Acts. I believe Acts 2:42-47 is an effective church model for all generations. These verses outline principles, not practices. When the principles are right a church can then align its practices to fit these principles. This, in essence, becomes the core values of the church. The first century church was dealing with a multi-generational, multi-cultural population. The miracle of Pentecost was the fact Jews and Gentiles from across the Empire heard the message of God in their own language. These people were vastly different in customs, preferences, and background. Yet, they came together around principles that led to a church that grew exponentially over the next months and years. This all happened in the face of severe criticism, push-back from the religious establishment and great persecution. What allowed the church to thrive under these conditions? The answer is simple. The Holy Spirit of God rallied these early Believers around a set of principles that shaped them into a mighty army proclaiming a life changing message. The results were phenomenal.

The good news is these principles still work today. The key is a willingness to shape ministry and practice around these timeless truths. Eight simple words can literally reshape, renew, and revive a church. They are:

Commitment. The early church was committed to learning and remaining committed to the teachings and practices of Christ as revealed in the Apostles Doctrine. "And they continued steadfastly in the Apostles doctrine…" (Vs. 42a) Jesus had promised to bring a Helper to cause them to remember all He said and did. "But the Helper, the Holy Spirit, whom the Father will send in My name, He will teach you all things, and bring to your remembrance all things that I said to you." (John 14:26) The church formed its mission around the teachings of Christ.

A church will be either structure centered or mission centered. In a structure centered church the focus can be on many things. It can be programs, tradition, maintaining the status quo, power groups, the past, organization, budgets, preferences, differences, and a host of other things. Not all of these are necessarily bad, but when they become the driving force behind what they do, they will hinder the church from being as effective as it can and should be.

A mission centered church is one that, through a study of Scripture, answers questions such as; According to the life and teachings of Christ what should our church look like? What should be our main focus? When the church comes to understand the mission of Christ for the church and then is willing to adopt His mission as the church's mission it is then ready to structure or re-structure everything around this very important principle. I believe the Believers in the First Church of Jerusalem spent a lot of time digging into all that Jesus had said the church was to be and do. They came out ready to be that church and to do His Will. Their preferences, differences, and structure took a back seat to the will of Christ. To learn what they took from their doctrinal studies, look at how the church behaved. Everything that follows in Acts 2 is a result, I believe, of their continuation in the Word.

The tough questions for the church are these: Is there a willingness on the part of the church membership to trade structure for mission? Is the church willing to make the changes necessary to be mission centered? Will the church trade a "hold on" mindset" for a "visionary mindset"?

In order for a church to become a mission centered church, it must look forward much more than it looks back. Success never comes from living life looking in the rear view mirror. Can you imagine someone driving a car while looking primarily through the rearview mirror rather than the windshield? I don't want to be on the road with that person. I can assure you there is going to be a major wreck. Every church that has existed for any length of time has a history. That history may be good, bad, or mixed. In a church where the history is good this history should be celebrated. At the same time care must be taken where the mission statement becomes, "Remember when..." In a church where the history is not so good, mistakes should be learned from, but the events of the past cannot be allowed to stand in the way of the mission for the future. Paul's commitment must become the commitment of the church. "Brethren, I do not count myself to have apprehended; but one thing *I do*, forgetting those things which are behind and reaching forward to those things which are ahead," (Philippians 3:13).

Unity. "...fellowship, in the breaking of bread," (Vs 42b). As the church determined its mission by it became a very united church that was known for its fellowship. Around the Lord's Table and in the daily activities of the church, there was a spirit of oneness. Remember, this was a very diverse congregation and a rapidly growing congregation; yet, there was incredible unity.

When the mission is the most important, the church will be more suited for unity. Most disagreements in church are not over the mission of the church; they are over the structure of the church. People fuss over things like the location of classrooms, who is going to be in charge, and other things that are not central to the mission of the church.

The goal is not unity for unity sake. The goal is unity for the cause of Christ. People must be willing to lay aside their preferences, personal agendas, and differences, so the cause of Christ can be elevated and carried out. How does a church remain united when there are so many different personalities and opinions in the congregation? Unity is derived when the main thing remains the main thing. The main thing is "Jesus." A church is in trouble when pet beliefs, personal agendas, and peripheral issues get in the way of a focus on Jesus and His commands to the church. Satan loves to divide the family of God. Jesus said, "And if a house is divided against itself, that house cannot stand." (Mark 3:25) When Satan can bring division into the church the witness of Christ is greatly harmed. On the other hand, where there is unity around the person, message and mission of Christ that church is empowered in its witness.

Prayer. "...and in prayers." (Vs 42c) A primary activity of the First century church was prayer. There is no substitute for prayer in the church. A study of Acts reveals prayer was central to everything the church did. When confronted with persecution they prayed; when determining who to send out as missionaries they prayed; when boldness was needed to witness they prayed; when structuring the church they prayed; when they needed power they prayed. This principle is timeless. When asked how to revitalize a church that is struggling my first answer is gather a group of praying people together and begin to seek God in the matter. Do nothing before you pray. Once you have prayed, pray some more, then move at His command.

I believe today there are strongholds in the church that are holding it back. These strongholds are crippling and even killing churches. While this sounds very negative, I also believe we have a God who can pull down strongholds. The Scripture says, "For the weapons of our warfare are not carnal but mighty in God for pulling down strongholds," (2 Corinthians 10:4). I have seen churches, where people have said, "There is no hope for that church," become revitalized and make a huge impact for Christ in the community and the world. People stopped trying to change things in the flesh, started praying, and the mighty power of God pulled down strongholds that had existed for years. Only God can do that.

I am grateful I grew up in a church where I witnessed the power of God at work in prayer. I remember Sunday nights in this small church, in rural South Georgia, where people would come together to pray. I mean they meant business in prayer. They cried out to God for the church and the community. They asked God to do things that were so large only He could take the credit. Guess what happened? God moved and He moved powerfully. People were saved, and the church became one of the leaders in Evangelism. This was in a county of less than 18,000 people. God revitalized His church. This greatly influenced my ministry. When I became pastor, I didn't know anything else to do, but to call the people to pray for God to do something bigger than we as the church could ever imagine! He did, and more importantly He will do the same today!

Expectancy. "Then fear came upon every soul, and many wonders and signs were done through the apostles. (Vs. 43) The Believers in the Jerusalem church expected things to happen! They believed God would do great things, and He did. Where is expectancy in the church today? Too many people come to church expecting nothing much to happen and they are not surprised. Why is this so sad but so true? Because nothing has been done to prepare the church for great things to happen? Where is the prayer, the unity, the mission, or the vision? One of my memories as a pastor was a time when the church was seeing a substantial number of people come to Christ. Baptisms were taking place every service, every Sunday. One Sunday, in one of the services, there was no one to baptize. I remember one church member saying to me something like this, "Wow, I felt something was missing today. We didn't baptize." At first I was a little defensive, but then I realized people were coming to church expecting things to happen. I celebrated this attitude! Too often the church is thrown by the terms "signs and wonders." I believe this can be translated for the church today as expectancy for God to do miraculous things!

Generosity. "Now all who believed were together, and had all things in common, and sold their possessions and goods, and divided them among all, as anyone had need." (Vs 44-45.) Selfishness was not a characteristic of the majority of the first century believers. They were a sacrificial congregation.

There is a principle called the "Pareto" principle. It is the 80/20 rule. In church it translates this way: 80% of the ministry is done by 20% of the people. 80% of the financial support for local ministry and world missions is given by 20% of the people. On the other hand 80% of the complaints come from 20% of the people, normally very powerful people. Imagine what could happen if this were not true. I believe a perfect example of what could happen if a majority of the Body of Christ became committed to the ministry and mission of Jesus as seen in the first century church. They were sold out to Christ.

What would happen in today's church if a majority of church members were faithful stewards of their giftedness and financial gifts? What if the church became serious about generosity? I believe we could see results like those seen in first century Christianity. A church serving together and giving together can greatly impact the world with the Gospel.

Celebration. "So continuing daily with one accord in the temple, and breaking bread from house to house, they ate their food with gladness and simplicity of heart," (Vs. 46). The first century church met daily, not once a week. When they met they celebrated the Resurrection of Christ. The primary issue isn't when the church meets; the primary issue is, what happens when it meets? I believe in reverence, times of solemn assembly, and quiet reflection over who God is and all God has done. I also believe in celebration. When the church meets it meets to celebrate a risen Lord, not mourn a dead Savior.

Salvation is by the Grace of God and comes through Repentance and Faith. his is the message of the church. People are not saved based on feelings or the lack of feelings. They are saved based on what they do with Christ. With that said, I do believe worship brings with it emotion. God created us body, soul, and spirit. "Now may the God of peace Himself sanctify you completely; and may your whole spirit, soul, and body be preserved blameless at the coming of our Lord Jesus Christ." (I Thessalonians 5:23) I believe God created emotion. I wouldn't want a God that didn't bring out an emotional response. I believe the first century worship was alive! I believe what happened in worship in the Temple spilled over into life outside the Temple. Acts 2:46 says as much. There was gladness in the early church.

I believe a great testimony to a church is when someone says, "There is something special in that place." A church characterized by gladness will be contagious. In fact it will lead to the next principle that was very evident in the Jerusalem church.

Community. "Praising God and having favor with all the people." (Acts 2:47a)

This may sound like a strange word when it comes to the church, but I believe it is a very accurate word. As the early church expressed commitment to God's Word, demonstrated unity and generosity, prayed, and worshiped, God honored them and blessed them. They were given favor with the Jewish community in Jerusalem who were not Believers in Christ. Their approach was very attractive to the common person.

When I am asked for steps that need to be taken for revitalization to take place, I often answer this way. "One of the primary things you need to do is to repair your reputation with the community if it needs repair. Or you may need to build a reputation with the community." When it comes to reputation there are three categories. A church may have a positive reputation, a negative reputation, or be invisible. Someone posed a question to me some time ago I can't get away from. It was this, "If the doors of your church closed tomorrow, how long before anyone would know? More importantly, would anybody care?" What a church does inside its walls affects its reputation. A church that is known for fighting, running off the pastor, or being

51

snobby will have a poor reputation in the community. Even a facility that isn't kept well communicates negatively. A church doesn't have to have expensive facilities, but they should have clean neat facilities. What the church does or doesn't do outside its walls can cause it to be invisible. The early church was a church without walls! This means more than a lack of permanent meeting space. It means they existed more for the people who were outside the church; not only for those on the inside. The church can never allow those who are on the inside to prevent them from reaching those who are on the outside.

A church needs to take a hard look at its reputation. It needs to be an honest look. If there needs to be repentance, then the church needs to repent. Whatever needs to be done, to restore or build a reputation with the community that is Christ honoring, must take place. There must be a no excuse mentality when it comes to connecting with the community. A positive community connection opens the door to the final principle.

Evangelistic. "And the Lord added to the church daily those who were being saved." (Vs 47b) There is no mistaking the fact the first century church was an evangelistic church. It is interesting to watch how this church grew. Acts 2:47 said, "people were added daily." That is impressive, but that is only the beginning. By the time you reach Acts 6 the church is being multiplied. "Now in those days, when the number of the disciples was multiplying..." From addition to multiplication; now that is impressive!

Let's go back to verse 42. Can you envision the early Believers gathering and discussing their doctrine? Someone asks, "What was the main emphasis of our Lord's ministry?" Someone replies, "People. He was all about people. There was the time when He engaged in conversation with a Samaritan woman at a well." With surprise on his face another Believer asks, "Do you mean Jesus talked with a non-Jewish woman with a horrible reputation in the middle of the day?" They replied, "Not only did He speak with her, He led her to trust in Him as the Messiah, the Savor. In fact, that is one of the reasons our people crucified Him. They could not handle the fact He dealt with 'unclean' people."

Everything we do should be so people who don't know Christ can know Him. That is the reason the church exists. Small, large, rural, suburban, or urban doesn't matter. The church exists to get the Gospel to the world. The church can never allow those who are on the inside to prevent us from reaching those who are outside the church. Unfortunately, in the modern church, much of what is done is done for those who are already Believers. We exchange Believers from one church to another and think we are fulfilling the Great Commission. The Great Commission is about "making disciples" not "swapping disciples." You cannot read the New Testament and not be convinced Jesus, the New Testament writers, and the church were all about making sure people heard the Gospel and had opportunity to respond to it. This is what we should be like today. The church must be willing to adopt a strategy that is Evangelistic. The church cannot be content with doing business as usual. Commitment, unity, prayer, generosity, expectancy, celebration, and community efforts should lead to an intentional sharing of the Gospel. That is the picture of a church experiencing revitalization.

Chapter 3

A CHURCH IN TRANSITION

Joshua 1:1-1:9

We are living in some of the best of days and some of the most challenging of days when it comes to American Christianity and the local church. The church life which existed thirty years ago will no longer suffice as a vibrant healthy church today. What drew the masses in the 1970's will no longer compel potential church members to your church and ministries. I was in Oklahoma City a few days ago speaking at a conference on church revitalization and renewal and as the final speaker of the closing evening, I asked those in attendance which made up over 180 individual churches represented, if they "loved their grandchildren and children enough to make the necessary changes within their church to bring them back to the Lord?" There was a moment of silence and eventually a long drawn out moan by some of the participants because the question actually hit too close to those in attendance and their local expression of church.

Many made expressions that they indeed would make the necessary decisions and changes to allow their local church to become more inclusive towards the younger generations. When it was all over a lady cornered me in the back of the church where we were meeting and wanted me to know that even though their church was made up of only old people, they were the ones holding true to the scripture and were the remnant clinging to the things of old and if a younger group of individuals wanted to become part of their church, they would need to adopt and adapt to what the church was already doing. I asked if she went to a large church and she sighed that they were once quite large but now they were only a handful of participants, but they were very committed to one another. I was left with the impression from that church and this dear saintly individual that they had embraced the philosophy that stated: "Would the last one left alive, please turn the lights off?" I found an interesting article entitled: "Age changes things."

Who changed everything when I wasn't looking? I've noticed lately that everything is farther away than it used to be. It's even twice as far to the corner now, and they've added a hill! I've given up running for the bus; it leaves much earlier than it used to. And it seems to me that they are making the stairs steeper than in the old days, and have you noticed the smaller print the newspapers and magazines are now using? And there's no sense in asking anyone to read aloud anymore, as everyone speaks so softly that I can hardly hear them. The material in clothes are so skimpy now, especially around the waist and hips, and the way they size the clothes is much smaller than it used to be. Why, I have to buy clothes two sizes larger than what I wear just so they will fit me right! Even people are changing. They are so much younger than they used to be when I was their age. On the other hand, people my own age are much older than I am. I ran into an old classmate of mine the other day, and she had aged so much that she didn't recognize me! I got to thinking about my poor dear friend while I was combing my hair this morning, and in doing so, I glanced at my own reflection in the mirror.... Really now! They don't even make good mirrors anymore. So tell me now... Who changed things?[13]

You have probably heard the quote, *"The good ole days were not so good."* Our memory has a tendency to remember things in a way that makes us feel good, and maybe isn't necessarily true to reality. Selective memories have a way of distorting reality. As a matter of fact, most of us think that our churches are okay.

---

[13] **http://www.agelessfx.com/funny_getting_older_jokes.html.**

Statistically however, we see that this is not true. Did you know that:

- There are 344,000 protestant evangelical churches from the eight mainline denominations in the western hemisphere, which are in plateau and decline.
- 95% of all churches in North America average 100 or less.
- Over 82% of American churches are in decline or on a plateau.
- Each year 3,500 to 4,000 churches die in North America (900 last year within our Denomination alone).
- Studies have shown that churches typically plateau in attendance by their fifteenth year, and by year 35 they begin having trouble replacing the members they lose.
- They have the inability to regain the critical mass necessary to regrow the church utilizing the tools and techniques they are presently employing.
- 50 – 60 churches in North America close their door every week.
- A more recent series of studies (The State of the Church) was conducted by Bill Day; Associate Director of the *Leavell Center for Evangelism and Church Health*, who serves the New Orleans Baptist Theological Seminary as the Gurney Professor of Evangelism and Church Health in his sequential studies on church health and growth of 2003, 2007, and 2010 where he reports that currently there are less than seven percent (6.8) of our SBC churches which are healthy growing churches. That means 3,087 of our 45,727 SBC churches are healthy.

So you can see that the church today all across America is in a time of transition.

Where I minister in central Florida, some local churches are transitioning from pastor to pastor in an attempt to fix the declining participation within their fellowship. In a day where we have some of the best and most efficient conveniences to give back time to the American populace, we have church memberships which seem unable to mount the necessary volunteers to carry on the work of the church because everyone has replaced available time with other commitments which take them away for the local church. It is a day of transition for sure. But there are some churches which are transitioning to the changes that must be made in order for us to continue to be faithful to the Great Commission.

Understanding that things change is biblical. J. Oswald Sanders writes in his book *Spiritual Leadership*: *"A work originated by God and conducted on spiritual principles will climb above the shock of a change of leadership and indeed will probably thrive better as a result."*[14] Let us look at how God's early church embraced a change that enabled them to receive the promises of God. Open the Word of God and read with me Joshua 1:1-9:

After the death of Moses the LORD's servant, the LORD spoke to Joshua son of Nun, who had served Moses: "Moses My servant is dead. Now you and all the people prepare to cross over the Jordan to the land I am giving the Israelites. I have given you every place where the sole of your foot treads, just as I promised Moses. Your territory will be from the wilderness and Lebanon to the great Euphrates River—all the land of the Hittites and west to the Mediterranean Sea. No one will be able to stand against you as long as you live. I will be with you, just as I was with Moses. I will not leave you or forsake you. "Be strong and courageous, for you will distribute the land I swore to their fathers to give them as an inheritance. Above all, be strong and very courageous to carefully observe the whole instruction My servant Moses commanded you. Do not turn from it to the right or the left, so that you will have success wherever you go. This book of instruction must not depart from your mouth; you are to recite it day and night so that you may carefully observe everything written in it. For then you will prosper and succeed in whatever you do. Haven't I commanded you: be strong and courageous? Do not

---

[14] Spiritual Leadership, p. 132.

> *be afraid or discouraged, for the* LORD *your God is with you wherever you go."*[15]

I would like to draw your attention to the five things a church in transition must do:

I. A church in transition must *deal with its past*. (1-2)

Max Lucado in his book *In the Eye of the Storm* tells a story of Chippie the parrot.

> Chippie was just purchased by a proud owner. She wanted to take good care of Chippie. To show her love she decided to clean Chippie's cage. She started from the top and worked her way down to the bottom. She started cleaning the bottom of the cage using a vacuum cleaner. The phone rang and instinctively she answered it. Paying no attention to her hose on the vacuum. When she heard whoosh. She looked, and her worst fears were confirmed. She had sucked Chippie into the vacuum. In a panic she turns the vacuum off, opens it up to find Chippie in the middle of the bag covered in dust and dirt. Immediately she picks him up and rushes to the bathroom sink. She turns on the water and immerses him. Believing she has done the right thing to clean him up, she now looks at him and realizes that he is shivering and soaked. Realizing where she is and recognizing what is available, she picks up her hair dryer and turns it on high. A reporter gets wind of the incident. After the interview he asks,

---

[15] The Holy Bible: Holman Christian Standard Version. (Nashville: Holman Bible Publishers, 2009), Jos 1:1–9.

"So how's Chippie?" The owners reply, "Chippie doesn't sing much anymore."[16]

Neither do we when we have been "sucked in, washed up, and blown away." We all have been. However, when this happens to us, it is important that we become like the jockey hired by a Kentucky horse farmer.

You see there were these two Kentucky horse farmers who raced each other once a year. This race very competitive and they both wanted to win so badly. One year one of the farmers found a jockey to ride his horse. This professional jockey filled his farmer so with hopes of winning the big race. The race was off and running. It was a muddy day. They were neck and neck all the way until the last turn. That is when one slipped knocking both horses to the ground. The professional jockey gets back up, gets on the horse, does everything within his power and expertise as a jockey and wins the race.

He rides over to the owner who is mad. The jockey is so excited and says, "We won!" The owner says, "You don't know what you did do you?" The jockey replied, "I know that I fell. That happens, the important thing is that I got back up and on the horse finished the race and we won!" By this time the owner is mad enough to bite nails and screams, "You got back up and on the horse alright, but you got on the wrong horse!"

When we fall we often get back on the wrong horse. You have been there and so have I. There is the horse of anger. There is the horse of jealousy. There is the horse of pride. Some struggle with horse of wealth. Yet what we need to do is stop looking over our

---

[16] http://gcfirst.org/2012/10/08/my-favorite-max-lucado-story-chippie-the-parakeet/.

shoulder towards the past and get back up on the horse of God's leading towards victory and success.

Israel had to deal with it's past. *"Moses my servant is dead."* Can you imagine the Israelites feelings? Here is their great leader Moses who has led them time after time after time for forty years out of the challenges they faced and he is gone. Here is the leader the Lord God used to release them from their Egyptian bondage and he is no longer there to lead the people. Here is the one who supplied their most basic of needs and fed them daily has past. The great and influential leader Moses who was led by the Lord God in heaven to do all kinds of incredible miracles is now dead. Yet even in the midst of this reality and challenge, God declares it is time to deal with their past. For if you look clearly and sense God's divinely inspired word, the Lord was declaring in this moment in time: *"Hear me my dear children of Israel, it was not the mere man who was leading, it was I, the Lord your God who lead you, provided for you, and protected you all of those years."*

Church members tell me all over the country that their best days in a church were when Pastor Mighty was their pastor. It was almost as if they knew for sure that he had a great big "S" tattooed to his chest because they viewed him as their super pastor. He was able to leap tall buildings in a single bound and on it goes. But, have you ever stopped to consider that the work of Lord is not hindered by the decease or transition of His servants? No matter how well known that minister might be. No matter how long he has served as your pastor. No matter how the Lord has chosen to bless you and your church through this leader, when the local prophet of God is removed, God still has a plan and a way for you and your church to move forward to accomplish the tasks he has called you.

Matthew Henry in his commentary declares:

> Honor is here put upon Joshua, and great power lodged in his hand. God gives him wisdom, instruction, and encouragement. As the Lord had before

spoken to Moses concerning young Joshua,[17] but now he speaks to him, perhaps just as He spoke to Moses.[18] The Lord speaks to him quickly.[19]

Warren Wiersbe stresses that:

The point to be realized here is that God will change hands to show that whatever means He uses, He is not tied to any single channel. Leaders do not lead forever, even godly leaders like Moses. There comes a time in every ministry when God calls for a new beginning with a new generation and new leadership.[20]

Excluding Joshua and Caleb, the old former generation of Jews had completely perished during the wanderings of Israel in the wilderness. Now Joshua is commissioned to lead this new generation into a new challenge. It is the challenge of coming to and the conquering of the Promised Land. The scripture announces, *"God buries His workmen, but His work goes on."* It was the Lord God who had selected Joshua, and everybody within Israel knew that Joshua was indeed their new leader.

It is a sad statement on any local church when its membership depends so greatly on their leader, the under-shepherd of God, that when a transition takes place the church is crippled for a time. Over the years I have visited many churches which were floundering and practically destroying themselves in their pointless attempts to preserve the past and escape the future.

What we need to be depending on during those times and any time for that matter is a God who is seated in the Holy place and ready and able to lead his children to great and greater victories.

---

[17] C.f. Numbers 27:18.

[18] C.f. Leviticus 1.

[19] Matthew Henry, Matthew Henry's Commentary on the Whole Bible: Complete and Unabridged in One Volume (Peabody: Hendrickson, 1994), 289.

[20] Warren W. Wiersbe, Be Strong, "Be" Commentary Series (Wheaton, IL: Victor Books, 1996), 21.

What I have often seen is when a leader leaves, church members often create a crises of unbelief because they no longer have a shepherd. Yet, if you notice. here within this passage, the Lord God continues to call his children onward into the "promised land." Now notice all that the Lord God had already done:

- God had led Israel from Egypt to the desert.
- God had led Israel from the desert into the wilderness.
- God now wants to lead them from the wilderness to the crossing over of the Jordan River.

What I have noticed and I prayerfully hope you will notice is that all throughout this wonderful Book we know as the *Word of God* that God is leading His church to new horizons and new victories all the time.

One thing is clear and certain. Just like the Israelites, we cannot stay in Egyptian bondage and still cross over to the victories offered within the Promised Land. Listen dear child of God, it is when we look to the past and live in the past, that the past can actually defeat us and keep us from experiencing the great and wonderful blessings God has for each and everyone of us in the present. The first charge was to cross the Jordan. Verse 2 reads literally, *"Now arise, cross ..."* In my everyday jargon it means get moving and cross over immediately, stop delaying. It is the Lord Jesus Christ which lovingly commands this church and any church for that matter to follow.[21] It is when we are following that there is no room for procrastination.

If we are going to be obedient, we must follow God completely. I would tell my son a vital lesson I learned as a young minister, which is eighty percent obedience is still disobedience. That means we cannot stay where we are, we must faithfully move forward. Often I have prayed with and for godly Church Revitalizers who were criticized, persecuted, mistreated, and attacked simply because, like Joshua, they had a divine directive to lead a church into new fields of conquest and victory; but the people just would not follow. More

---

[21] C.f. Luke 9:59–62.

than one renewal pastor has been offered as a sacrificial lamb because he dared to suggest that the declining church make some necessary changes. I usually ask congregations if they love their grandchildren enough so they would be willing to make the necessary changes to bring them and their parents back into their church.

There are many which the Lord is beckoning to move forward, yet it is their past, which is tying them down, holding them up, burdening them beyond measure and they need to deal with it. Mourning the death of a great leader is natural and it is the grace of the Lord which allows us to deal with such passing. We are allowed those moments of grief and sadness. We are able to mourn our past times where we were out of proper fellowship with God because of our sins. But, there comes a time when the Lord wants us to deal with all of these and move on.

Now you might know that Joshua was from the tribe of Ephraim,[22] and lived 110 years.[23] In the Book of Numbers, Moses renamed young Joshua from Hoshea.[24] The name Joshua means "The LORD is salvation." The name later became yēšûa where in the Greek we get Iēsous, and the English, 'Jesus'. In this passage of Numbers Chapter 13 thirty eight years earlier Joshua had explored with the other eleven spies this land and declared it good and fruitful. I see remembering in his mind just how beautiful and fertile the land was. But now, Joshua has a new charge and a new challenge. He will lead the Israelites to conquer this very land, which the Lord promised. It is in this very commissioning of Joshua that he is challenged and charged to accomplish three things. He is to lead the people into the land. He is to defeat the enemy they encounter. He is to claim the inheritance, which God had promised so long ago.

When you stop for a moment to think about it, God could have done this in many other ways. The Lord could have just in a snap of a finger carried out all that was required for Israel to possess the land. God could have chosen to rain down thunder so loud that the enemies fled for their lives. The Holy One could have sent one of His angels

---

[22] C.f. Numbers 13:8.

[23] C.f. Joshua 24:29.

[24] C.f. Numbers 13:16.

to accomplish the task. But the Lord our God chose to use a man by the name of Joshua instead. All of the powers necessary to accomplish the task were made available to this new leader for all to see.

A church in transition must *Deal with it's past*.

II. A church in transition must *develop His plan*. (3-6)

President Ulysses S. Grant was taken to a golf course one day. A golfer wanted him to experience what golf was all about. The golfer went into extensive explanations of the swing. Then he wanted to model the golf swing for President Grant. He teed up the ball, swung, and missed the ball completely taking a huge divot and leaving the ball in place. He repeated this three times. On the third time the President said, "This game seems exciting, but I am not sure what the ball is for."[25]

We need to discover what the ball is for and understand the plan. To develop God's plan we first must:

Find His strategy and plan (Joshua 1:3-4).

I have given you every place where the sole of your foot treads, just as I promised Moses. Your territory will be from the wilderness and Lebanon to the great Euphrates River —all the land of the Hittites — and west to the Mediterranean Sea.[26]

Since Joshua had a threefold task to accomplish, God gave him three special promises, one for each task. First, God would empower Joshua to cross the river and claim the land. Secondly He would

---

[25] **http://thegolfguru.hubpages.com/hub/Golf-Quotes—-US-Presidents.**

[26] The Holy Bible: Holman Christian Standard Version. (Nashville: Holman Bible Publishers, 2009), Joshua 1:3–4.

embolden Joshua so he could defeat the enemy. The last of the three special promises God gave Joshua was that he was to allocate the land to each tribe as its inheritance. God did not give Joshua explanations, He expected, that when one trusts God's promises and steps out in faith, one could be sure that the Lord will give them the directions needed when they need them.

The Lord within this passage of scripture had already given them the territory. But they had not discovered it yet. They had to find where God was working. Listen my dear Church, God has already given us things, but we still have to find them and develop them.

Secondly, we need to finish His design and plan.

No one will be able to stand against you as long as you live. I will be with you, just as I was with Moses. I will not leave you or forsake you (v.5).[27]

They were promised, *"No man shall be able to stand..."* Did this mean that there would not be a war? No. It meant that God would provide victory! Forty years earlier, the people of Israel wavered in faith because their spies had seen great warriors in Canaan. Now those warriors had not gone away and had not lost any of their military powers. But Joshua and Israel would have success against them, because the Lord was promising that He would cause them to flee. The enemies of Israel could not succeed because God was greater than those enemies. Listen dear church, just like Israel's enemies would be ineffective, (vs.5) the world will be ineffective if we walk closely with the Lord.

As God was with Moses, so He would be with Joshua: *"I will not leave you nor forsake you"* (v. 5).

Did you know that this very promise was repeated to others in the scripture? It was promised to Solomon in 1 Chronicles 28:20:

---

[27] The Holy Bible: Holman Christian Standard Version. (Nashville: Holman Bible Publishers, 2009), Jos 1:5.

> *Then David said to his son Solomon, "Be strong and courageous, and do the work. Don't be afraid or discouraged, for the LORD God, my God is with you. He won't leave you or forsake you until all the work for the service of the LORD's house is finished."*

It was given to each one of us in the New Testament. For in Hebrews 13:5-6 it says:

> *Your life should be free from the love of money. Be satisfied with what you have, for He Himself has said, I will never leave you or forsake you. Therefore, we may boldly say: The Lord is my helper; I will not be afraid. What can man do to me?*

What we need to understand is that leaders do change and times they are changing. But can I tell you the greatest news today? The greatest news for each and every one of us is that God changes not. As a believer we are told we should have courage (vs. 6–7, 9). The exciting thing about this requirement is that the great provider through the Word of God provides this much-needed courage.

> *This book of instruction must not depart from your mouth; you are to recite it day and night so that you may carefully observe everything written in it. For then you will prosper and succeed in whatever you do (Joshua 1:8).*

For you see the commands and promises found within verses 2–9 set out the covenant relationship between God and His people. On God's side, He chose Israel to inherit the land (v. 6). On Israel's side, they must now by faith claim the gift (vs. 3–4). It is not so much a matter of obedience to cross the Jordan, important as that is, as a matter of trust in God (vs. 6–7, 9). The Lord gives the Israelites a reason to trust Him. He promises His divine presence will be with them (vs. 5, 9b). Likewise the trusting church obeys our Lord's command to evangelize the world:

*Then Jesus came near and said to them, "All authority has been given to Me in heaven and on earth. Go, therefore, and make disciples of all nations, baptizing them in the name of the Father and of the Son and of the Holy Spirit, teaching them to observe everything I have commanded you. And remember, I am with you always, to the end of the age" (*Matthew. 28:18–20*).*

We are not promised peace as the world knows it, but we are promised the peace of God in the midst of any crisis. Our calling is not one of ease, but one of endurance. The lesson for God's people and His church today is clear: God has given us *"all spiritual blessings ... in Christ"* (Eph. 1:3), and we must step out by faith and claim these blessings. The Lord our God has set before His church an open door that nobody can close (Rev. 3:8), and we must walk through that door by faith and claim new territory for the Lord.

It is impossible to stand still in the Christian life and service for when you stand still, you immediately start going backwards. *"Let us go on!"* is God's challenge to His church (Hebrews 6:1), and that means moving ahead into new territory. In other words, the writer is not talking about self-effort; he is appealing to use to yield ourselves to the power of God, the same power that upholds the whole universe. How can we fall when God is holding us?

So what more could we desire than what God has said to you in Joshua 1:5? *If God be for you, who can be against you?* Look away from yourself, from your enemies, from your difficulties, unto Him who hath said *"I will not fail thee, nor forsake thee."* As Christ followers we can count upon Him, and His strength will displace our weakness. His strength will displace our fears and replace it with courage.

3. Have Faith in His provisions and plan. (6)

Moses' greatness was not due to Moses, but to the Lord. In the same way Joshua had nothing to worry about with Moses gone, because the Lord was not gone. It is no accident that the Lord told

Joshua to *"be strong and of good courage"* immediately after promising never to leave nor forsake him (vv. 5–6).

Joshua could be strong and of good courage because God is with Him and God is giving this land to Israel. Joshua must have unwavering faith in God's plan. When we start implementing God's plan, the going will get rough. We must have faith that God will do what He said He would do.

Before God could fulfill His promises, Joshua had to exercise faith and *"be strong and of good courage"* (1:6). God's sovereign Word is an encouragement to God's servants to believe God and obey His commands.

The lesson for God's people today is clear: God has given us *"all spiritual blessings ... in Christ"* (Eph. 1:3), and we must step out by faith and claim them. He has set before His church an open door that nobody can close (Rev. 3:8), and we must walk through that door by faith and claim new territory for the Lord.

It is impossible to stand still in Christian life and service for when you stand still, you immediately start going backward. *"Let us go on!"* is God's challenge to His church (Heb. 6:1), and that means moving ahead into new territory.[28]

As Charles Spurgeon put it, Joshua:

"was not to use the promise as a sofa upon which his idleness might indulge, but as a girdle to gird up ones loins for future activity."[29]

> In short, God's promises are prods, not pillows. God's promises are given to encourage us to do with all our hearts and might whatever He has called us to do. A church in transition must *Deal with it's past.* A church in transition must *Develop His plan.*

---

[28] Warren W. Wiersbe, Be Strong, "Be" Commentary Series (Wheaton, IL: Victor Books, 1996), 24.

[29] Metropolitan Tabernacle Pulpit, vol. 14, p. 97.

III. A church in transition must discover His power (v. 7).

The end of verse 7 says, *"that you may prosper wherever you go."* Joshua discovered God's power. God prospers His people by allowing them to experience His power. How do we prosper? We prosper when we do what Joshua did. We prosper when we <u>obey God's word</u>, and we do not turn from it at all! God told Moses what to do, God told Joshua what to do, and God will tell each and every one of us what we are to do!

IV. A church in transition must *determine His doctrines and principles* (v.8).

> *This book of instruction must not depart from your mouth; you are to recite it day and night so that you may carefully observe everything written in it. For then you will prosper and succeed in whatever you do.*[30]

Israel was able to determine God's principles. The Lord's promises to Joshua did not mean that he and the people had no responsibilities. In these verses, the Lord strongly cautions Joshua to *"observe to do according to all the law."* He was not to deviate from it in any way (v. 7), but rather was to <u>keep it in his mouth and on his mind</u> (v. 8). Furthermore, he was to do *"all"* that was written in the law (v. 8). We need to remember that in the world in which we live, that the Lord our God is not satisfied with only partial obedience!

The Lord explicitly tied obedience to success in these verses (v. 8b). The God who had promised to give the Israelites the land <u>would not do so</u> apart from their total obedience. The experience of their fathers forty years earlier gave grim testimony to the importance of obedience. There can be no doubt that Joshua was possessed with a spirit of obedience to the Lord.

If we desire to discover and determine God's principles we must:

---

[30] The Holy Bible: Holman Christian Standard Version. (Nashville: Holman Bible Publishers, 2009), Joshua 1:8.

1. Grasp His word. *"This book of the Law shall not depart from your mouth."* In order for us to determine God's principles we must spend time in His word. We must read it in order to understand it.
2. Ponder His word. *"Meditate day and night."* The second step is to meditate. Meditation causes us to think about what God is saying. To take it to heart, allowing our minds to be transformed and renewed.

> *"But thou shalt meditate therein day and night, that thou mayest observe to do according to all that is written therein" (Joshua 1:8 KJV)*

Meditation upon the Word of God is one of the most important of all the means of grace and growth spiritually, there can be no true progress towards godliness without it.

Meditation on the divine things of God is not optional but required. It is something, which the Lord has commanded us to do. The command from the Lord, which Joshua received, was not restricted to Joshua alone, but it was addressed to all of God's people. Notice from the Word of God that this was not a one-time recommendation or command from the Lord.

> Deuteronomy 32:46 says we are to: *"Set your hearts unto all the words which I testify among you this day."*

> Proverbs 4:26 declares: *"Ponder the path of thy feet."*

> Haggai the prophet says: *"Consider your ways"* (Hag. 1:7).

> Luke 9:44 cries: *"Let these sayings sink down into your ears,"* which they cannot do, unless they be frequently turned over in our minds.

Philippians 4:8 pronounces: *"Whatsoever things are true, venerable, just, pure, lovely ... think on these things."*

Romans 12:2 shouts: *"Do not be conformed to this age, but be transformed by the renewing of your mind, so that you may discern what is the good, pleasing, and perfect will of God."*

3. Apply His word. To determine God's principles is totally meaningless if we do not apply them to our lives. It is an act of futility unless we carry them out. James says: *"be ye doers of the word and not hearers only."*

V. A church in transition must develop through His purpose (v.9).

Have you ever noticed in scripture that when God gives a command, He often accompanies it with a promise? Here the Lord assures Joshua a lifetime of continuous victory over his enemies, based on His unfailing presence and help. The words *"I will never leave you."* (Josh. 1:9) may be rendered, *"I will not drop or abandon you."*
Listen my dear church, God never walks out on His promises and His faithful churches. Our purpose as a church and as Christ followers is to be motivated by the Lord's command. Who is sending us? *"Have not I commanded you?"* The Israelites were not merely motivated by Joshua, it was God who was inspiring, stirring, and moving them.

1. Our purpose as a church and as individual Christ followers is strengthened by His commission.

"Have not I commanded you?" For remember it was Jesus who said, *"Go into all the world."* Dear church family we are not nor should we ever be affected by what others in the world and not in the church say or think.

2. Our purpose as a church and as individual Christ followers is solidified by His Company.

Who is with us? When we gather, we unite in the promise that, *"if God is for us, who can be against us?"* This church and every other Bible believing church become motivated by His presence and for the Lord's purpose! Yet, before we move away from this idea may I ask you a personal question this day: *Have you dealt with your past?* Have you developed His plan? Have you discovered His power for your life? Have you determined His principles? Do you have His purpose? You can experience all these and even much more today!

Chapter 4

An Urgent Call

Matthew 9:36-38

"Then Jesus went about all the cities and villages, teaching in their synagogues, preaching the gospel of the kingdom, and healing every sickness and every disease among the people. But when He saw the multitudes, He was moved with compassion for them, because they were weary and scattered, like sheep having no shepherd." Then He said to His disciples, "The harvest truly is plentiful, but the laborers are few. Therefore pray the Lord of the harvest to send out laborers into His harvest." (Matthew 9:36-38 NKJV)[31]

*I*f you have an emergency situation involving danger or injury, the first thought is to call 911. No one calls this number unless the situation is serious, or that's the way it's supposed to work. Unfortunately it doesn't always work out that way. If you don't believe me just talk to 911 operators. Some of the stories seem too dumb to be true, but as you know, truth is stranger than fiction. It's like the lady who called an Oklahoma police department asking for officers to find her a date, or the man who took the designated driver rule one step too far. He called 911 and asked an officer to be

---

[31] Scripture quotations are taken from the New King James Version (Nashville, TN: Thomas Nelson, Inc., Publishers, 1979, 1980, 1982).

dispatched to drive him to buy alcohol. Then there is the man who called the fire department to report his house on fire. When asked for an address he replied, "Just look for the smoke." Thankfully these are exceptions to the rule. I have sat in the 911 center where I serve as Chaplain for the local fire and police department. I have heard the urgency in people's voices when they have called to report a medical, police, or fire emergency. They are requesting immediate help due to the seriousness of the situation.

Matthew 9:36-38 is like a 911 call. You can't read this passage without sensing the urgency in Jesus' words. He has been ministering in the cities and villages in the region around the Sea of Galilee. Historians tell us there were approximately 300 towns in the area with an average population of 15,000 each. The people were diverse in every way. Jesus ministered to them all. He saw two things: He saw a great need. He also saw a lack of people meeting the need. Those who should have met the spiritual needs of the citizens of that region were more interested in their structure than they were in doing something about spiritual emptiness. The local spiritual leaders were good at imparting knowledge and good at finding fault, but they weren't very good at caring for the souls of the people. Those who should have cared the most were exclusive and clueless. This is what Jesus meant when He said, "They were weary and scattered, like sheep having no shepherd."

Unfortunately, this is reflected in too many churches today. There is a lack of urgency in many churches. It is as if the church has forgotten its mission is that of Jesus, "To seek and to save that which is lost." Procedure has replaced passion; complacency has replaced compassion; an internal focus has replaced an external one. The church has built walls that separate it from the community, rather than taking down walls that will allow it to take the Gospel to the community. No wonder most churches are plateaued or declining.

There must be an urgency in the church today. As Jesus said, "The fields are white unto harvest." We don't have a harvest problem in America today. The truth is we have a labor problem. In most communities 80% or more of the population is un-churched. Even in communities where the church has experienced growth, the growth

74

has not kept up with the ever increasing un-churched population. What will it take for the church to have the urgency of Jesus? **First we must do what He says to do.** Look at the last verse we read (verse 38). "Therefore pray the Lord of the harvest to send forth laborers into His harvest." Do you see the solution Jesus gives to the problem? You may be tempted to say, "Yes, He said we are to pray for the Lost." Actually that is not what He said in this passage. Please don't misunderstand. I believe we are to pray for the lost. Unfortunately that doesn't happen as it should in the average church. Most prayer meetings consist largely of prayers for people with physical needs. Now, don't get me wrong. We should pray for the sick and the injured and the grieving. The Bible is very clear on this. Unfortunately that is where many prayer meetings start and end. When was the last time you were in a prayer meeting where the main focus was people who need Christ? What He pleads with us to do in this passage is to pray for people who will be burdened to the point they will do whatever it takes to see people come to Christ. When was the last time you heard of a church having a meeting solely committed to praying to "The Lord of the Harvest" for an army of people willing to do whatever it takes to take the Gospel to the world? The first questions shouldn't be have we done this before, or what will it cost, or will it make me uncomfortable? The most important questions are what are we doing that is pleasing to God, and are we mobilizing people who are carriers of the Gospel into the world where they live?

I do not believe you can separate prayer from evangelism. Study the book of Acts. Note how many times prayer was central to the activity of the church. Two very popular passages are Acts 1:8 and Acts 2: 1-12. In Acts 1:8 we are told that through the power of the Holy Spirit the Church will be a witness locally and globally. Acts 2 is the account of Pentecost. The Holy Spirit fell and thousands came to faith in Christ. But couched between these two great passages are three verses that are often overlooked. Look at (Acts 1: 12-14). "Then they returned to Jerusalem from the mount called Olivet, which is near Jerusalem, a Sabbath day's journey. And when they had entered, they went up into the upper room where they were staying: Peter, James, John, and Andrew; Philip and Thomas; Bartholomew and

75

Matthew; James the son of Alphaeus and Simon the Zealot; and Judas the son of James. These all continued with one accord in prayer and supplication, with the women and Mary the mother of Jesus, and with His brothers." You will notice a concerted effort of prayer preceded every other ministry of the church. Yet, we think we can skip prayer and move straight to activity and see God sized things take place. Another very important verse is (Acts 4:31) It says, "And when they had prayed, the place where they were assembled together was shaken; and they were all filled with the Holy Spirit, and they spoke the word of God with boldness." The first century church was bold in its ministry and its witness. Where did it start? It started in a prayer meeting. Through the power of God the church believed it could accomplish unbelievably big things for God. I have yet to see a church revitalized that did not make prayer a vital part of its ministry.

I learned this from a layman. I had the privilege of pastoring the same church for over 30 years. As a new and young pastor of this very old church I quickly became discouraged, because I thought things ought to be happening faster than they were happening. I will never forget the Sunday afternoon I visited with a layman from the church. Little did I know this visit would change the course of my life and the church. It started with a feeling I couldn't explain. That Sunday afternoon I really felt I needed to visit this particular church member. I really couldn't explain why; I just knew I needed to go. I was a little embarrassed as I said to him, "James, I don't really know why I am here today. All I know is the reason is more than a casual visit. I was shocked when he said, "I know exactly why you are here. God brought you here." "He did?" was my reply. It was then that he began to share his story. A story that detailed how God had awakened him early one morning with the conviction he was to start getting up one hour earlier every morning to pray for the church. He was to tell no one; just pray. A few weeks prior to my visit God had impressed on him the time was close when he could share this experience. It was then he shared with me that he believed God wanted to do something special through Hebron Church. He continued by telling me he believed God was showing Him that the church should have a vision that included reaching 200 in Sunday School and beyond. The statement that really caught my attention is when James said, "I believe our vision must include all Northeast Georgia." To say I was a little skeptical is an understatement. You see the church was in a town whose high school graduated only about 60 students that year. The church was running around 100 on Sunday morning, including 30-40 children who came in on our church bus. The annual church budget was about $25,000. My only question was "how?" My thinking was James must know about some program of which I am not aware. I was shocked when, rather than rolling out a program, he told me prayer was the answer. He challenged me that Sunday afternoon to ask a couple friends if they were willing to start meeting with us one night a week to pray for the church. Somewhat reluctantly I agreed. I remember the first person I asked. His name was Mark. I approached him this way. "Mark, you wouldn't want to meet with me on Thursday night to pray for our church would you?" I was a little surprised when he responded, "I would love to." While Mark was a committed believer I just wasn't yet convinced anyone would want to give up an evening to pray for our church. It was Mark's response God used to convict me that a couple of my laymen had more faith than did I at the time. These guys were ready to do something I had to be convinced to do. It was those prayer times on Thursday nights that changed a pastor and a church. It was at that altar God showed me I was to plant my life in this small church and trust God for the results. In these prayer times I was taught to love the people and be patient with them. I was given courage to lead the church in the direction God wanted to take it. It was during these prayer times God began to take down the walls of the church and open it to connecting with the community in a multitude of ways. From these prayer times came an evangelism strategy.

I could go on and on. God did so much through prayer. While the times and day changed, for the 33 years I was pastor of Hebron this prayer group continued. James moved to another city; he continued to be man of prayer. Mark was my prayer partner for the entire 33 years. He continues to lead the group to this day.

As Pastor and Expositor A.C. Dixon so aptly said, "When you organize you get what man can do. When you pray you get what God can do." [32] Matthew 9 is a reminder that without concerted prayer there will probably not be a strong burden to develop people for the fields that are white unto harvest.

We must see with His eyes. Matthew 9:36 says, "But when He saw the multitudes..." Unlike most people, including the very religious, Jesus really saw the people. The marginalized, the hurting, and the spiritually empty were seen by Jesus as people to be loved and reached with the Gospel. Until the church sees beyond its walls, change will never take place. Until people outside the church are as cared for as the people who are already in the church, the church will continue to decline. The mission of the church is the great commission. The great commission is about people not maintenance of the program of the church. Too often we are more interested in maintaining programs that no are no longer effective than we are in the people around the church who desperately need the love of Jesus.

How do you see people? I mean really see them? What about your neighbor, the people who drive by your church, the people who really have nothing tangible to offer the church, but who need the ministry of the church? I want to challenge you to pray a prayer. Before I do, I must caution you. You know how this type caution works if you watch the commercials on television; especially those related to medications. The advertiser will present you with a medication that has been developed for the problem you are experiencing. Then the next 30 seconds or so are spent telling you all the things the medication can possibly do to you. By the time they are done you think you may be better off with the illness itself. I must caution you about this prayer. Do not pray it if you want to remain comfortable in your Christianity apart from genuinely caring about the people who need Christ. Do not pray this prayer if you don't want to see your neighbor, co-worker, friend, or acquaintances the same way you have always seen them. What is this prayer you ask? It is a prayer that is very simple to speak, but when spoken in sincerity, changes you as an individual and you as a church member. The prayer is, "Lord, starting today, give me your eyes. I no longer want to see people through the lens of prejudice or apathy. I want to see people

---

[32] http://christian-quotes.ochristian.com/A.C.-Dixon-Quotes/.

the way you saw the people in the region of Galilee. I want renewed eyesight that will affect everything I do." If you will pray this prayer and mean it, you can become a catalyst for a changed church and a changed community.

We must love with His heart. Matthew 9:36 goes on to say, "He was moved with compassion for them, because they were weary and scattered, like sheep having no shepherd." Jesus was deeply moved by the state of the people. hey were weary from the teachings and doctrines of the Pharisees who were heavy on words and low on genuine care. They were "scattered" or divided by religion void of relationships. Like sheep with no shepherd they had no one to guide them. Those who should have provided that guidance were more interested in preserving their traditions than impacting people lives. Does that sound a lot like the church today? The teachings of the church will never be believable until the burden of the church is seen through the way it loves people. The primary ministry of the church doesn't happen inside the walls of the church. It happens in the community. It happens as the church reaches out to people with the love of Christ. When our daughter, Dana, who is now an adult, was nine years old she was diagnosed with a brain tumor. This was a life changing event for our family. We spent several weeks at Egleston Children's Hospital in Atlanta. While there we met many great people including doctors and nurses. My wife really connected with one of the nurses. Late one night she walked into our daughter's room and asked if she could talk. She started out by saying, "We have noticed something about you. You spend time with family members of patients who have few if any visitors. You cry with them, talk with them, and spend time with them while having to deal with your own daughter's illness. Why and how do you do it?" My wife's reply was simple, "I am nothing special, but I do have a relationship with Jesus Christ that won't allow me to ignore the hurts and needs of others." She went on to say, "We are very fortunate to have a loving family and loving church. It would be selfish of me not to give the same love to people who need it most. It wasn't long after we brought Dana home from the hospital that this nurse and her family started attending our church. Eventually the entire family was saved and became very involved in the ministry of the church. It is more than

79

cliché to say we are to be the hands, feet, eyes, and mouth of Jesus. People who love like Jesus attract others to Him.

There is an urgent need for the church to begin to function like Jesus. We must take down any and all walls that would prohibit us from doing so. As an individual Christian what are you willing to do in order that you may see with His eyes and love with His heart? What changes are you willing for the church to make in order to be like Jesus in the community? What traditions, programs, or attitudes need to go that may be getting in the way? Are you willing to pray until change takes place within the church? Only when we get serious about the fields that are white until harvest will we make a real difference.

Chapter 5

When It Is Time
to Renovate Your Church

2 Chronicles 29:1-10

*H*ave you ever had the opportunity to remodel and renovate your home? It is an amazing thing to embark on a revitalization strategy for ones home and to do the things necessary to renovate. I found an interesting story from a contractor over in London, England:

> A builder was telling his friend about a property they were renovating. He said: "Behind this wall, we found a skeleton with a gold medal round his neck." The friend was quite surprised that such a find had been discovered and he inquired further about the discovery. He asked his contractor friend:
>
> "What was written on the skeletons medal?" The builder replied: "Great Britain Hide and Seek Champion, 1891."

Not every renovation project goes exactly the way one plans.
I am blessed with the honor of leading the RENOVATE National Church Revitalization Conference.[33] It is a twice-yearly conference,

---

[33] For more information about the Renovate National Church Revitalization Conference go to: **www.renovateconference.org**.

which is held the first week of November in Orlando and the second week of March in Kansas City. Participants from all over the world take part in this event and we have representation from eight protestant evangelical denominations.

Have you ever taken the time to stop and consider the things which are necessary to begin to revitalize ones church? Those who have heard me speak on this issue of church revitalization and renewal know that I believe strongly, that if you are going to get involved in the revitalization, renewal, and re-strengthening of your church, you must be willing to invest a minimum of at least one thousand days in the effort. Even more important some time between those initial three years and an additional two years, you will see the sudden shifts, which will be the beginning of your churches turnaround.

Within scriptures, we have a place where we can learn the proper steps, which need to be taken in order to renovate and return the church to its previous splendor. Look with me as we read 2 Chronicles 29:1–11:

> *"Hezekiah was 25 years old when he became king and reigned 29 years in Jerusalem. His mother's name was Abijah daughter of Zechariah. 2 He did what was right in the LORD's sight just as his ancestor David had done. 3 In the first year of his reign, in the first month, he opened the doors of the LORD's temple and repaired them. 4 Then he brought in the priests and Levites and gathered them in the eastern public square. 5 He said to them, "Hear me, Levites. Consecrate yourselves now and consecrate the temple of Yahweh, the God of your ancestors. Remove everything impure from the holy place. 6 For our fathers were unfaithful and did what is evil in the sight of the LORD our God. They abandoned Him, turned their faces away from the LORD's tabernacle, and turned their backs on Him. 7 They also closed the doors of the portico, extinguished the lamps, did not burn incense, and did not offer burnt offerings in the holy place of the God of Israel. 8 Therefore, the wrath*

*of the LORD was on Judah and Jerusalem, and He
made them an object of terror, horror, and mockery,
as you see with your own eyes. 9 Our fathers fell
by the sword, and our sons, our daughters, and our
wives are in captivity because of this. 10 It is in my
heart now to make a covenant with Yahweh, the God
of Israel so that His burning anger may turn away
from us. 11 My sons, don't be negligent now, for the
LORD has chosen you to stand in His presence, to
serve Him, and to be His ministers and burners of
incense."³⁴*

Often while churches rush around and race around trying to renovate the church today it is easy to miss the things necessary to revitalize the church. There are some things within the church that are
broken and need to be *repaired*. There are some things within the
church that are missing that need to be *replaced*. There are some
things within the church that simply do not belong in a church that
need to be *removed*. There are some things within the church that
have been *neglected*. There are some things within the church that
need to be *recognized* as hurting the church's chances for growth
and health. We need to look at the need for God's restoration of the
church today. The Church in the Western Hemisphere and particularly in North America is in critical need of renovation and revitalization. The church of the past full of health and vigor is no longer that
same church and it is a mere shell of itself. Churches today all across
the west are in need of church revitalization and renewal. I want
to speak to you today on the subject: *When It Is Time to Renovate
Your Church?*

You may be thinking, "well is not the Lord's Church *"the body
of Christ?"* While we cannot fit in one sermon the needs of churches
all across North America, we can begin to look at some of the things,
which need to be done to fit our own. I want to challenge you and
remind you today that is my duty and it is your duty today to do

---

³⁴ The Holy Bible: Holman Christian Standard Version. (Nashville: Holman Bible
Publishers, 2009), 2 Chronicles 29:1–11.

83

everything within our ability and strength to bring about renewed health and vitality to this church through the preaching and many ministries He has led us to share with the community in which we serve. If there is anything or many things which are fragmented or fractured within this fellowship, it is our duty to restore them.

David S. Dockery and others in the Holman Bible Handbook state:

> The neglect of the temple under Ahaz (28:24) prompted Hezekiah to order the Levites to consecrate themselves and begin repair of the sanctuary. After sixteen days the Levites completed the task and opened the temple once again (29:1–17). After the Levites had cleansed the articles of worship, the king led the congregation in worship through offerings. The musical guilds functioned again as David had intended and performed the psalms of David and Asaph (29:18–30). After the people had atoned for their sins, they offered burnt and thank offerings so numerous that the Levites were requested to assist the overburdened priests. The sight and sounds of the temple brought great joy to the congregation (29:31–36).[35]

Hezekiah succeeded his father Ahaz on the throne of the Kingdom of Judah (2 Kings 18:1; 2 Chr. 29:1). He is described as a great King. He followed the example of his great-grandfather Uzziah. Look at verses one and two:

> *"Hezekiah was 25 years old when he became king and reigned 29 years in Jerusalem. His mother's name was Abijah daughter of Zechariah. 2 He did what was right in the LORD's sight just as his ancestor David had done."*

---

[35] David S. Dockery, Trent C. Butler, Christopher L. Church, et al., Holman Bible Handbook (Nashville, TN: Holman Bible Publishers, 1992), 283.

He was one of Judah's greatest kings and most devoted spiritual leaders. He repaired the temple and restored the true worship of Jehovah on a scale not seen before. He called the whole nation of Israel and Judah, to observe the Passover together, and he cleansed the land of all of its idols. Hezekiah was just the opposite of his wicked father (Ahaz) in every way. He began his reign by opening the doors to the house of God. The house of God had been polluted by all of the frills of sensual idol worship. He was the Lord's leader for this time in the journey and Hezekiah had a plan that would bring glory back to the temple.

Let's look at the two things he did when it was time to renovate the church:

I. We Must Repair What Is Fractured (vs. 3).

Hezekiah in the first year of his reign, in the first month, opened the doors of the house of the LORD, and repaired them. He repaired what was fractured. Here this young twenty-five year old king initiated the changes necessary to bring about revitalization. Right from the outset of his reign, he got moving without delay nor procrastination. This new king did what was required in order to bring about a healthy temple. If we are going to see the revitalization of our churches, we also must not delay and get busy doing the necessary things that are needed to bring about church revitalization and renewal to our churches.

Notice within this passage that the things, which were fractured, were the consequence of his father's reign.[36] Ahaz had taken various articles from the Temple of God. He fractured these articles; he shut the doors of the Temple of the Lord so that worship could no longer be carried out. Then Ahaz set up pagan altars to wicked gods all over Jerusalem. Then he made pagan shrines in every town of Judah for the offering of sacrifices to pagan gods. The anger of the Lord was aroused and the people of God suffered for it. When Hezekiah rose to the throne, he reopened the doors of the Temple of the Lord and repaired their fractures.

---

[36] C.f. 2 Chronicles 28: 24.

85

All across North America there are fractured churches. You can drive on almost any church street today and see examples of those fractures. Many a church today has fallen in love with the world at the expense of leaving the Lord. If we are going to repair today's churches, we must go back to the scriptures for the drafts and designs. I think today any church could discover what God intends for it from the Book of Acts. Look with me at Acts 2:42-47:

> *42 And they devoted themselves to the apostles' teaching, to the fellowship, to the breaking of bread, and to the prayers. 43 Then fear came over everyone, and many wonders and signs were being performed through the apostles. 44 Now all the believers were together and held all things in common. 45 They sold their possessions and property and distributed the proceeds to all, as anyone had a need. 46 Every day they devoted themselves to meeting together in the temple complex, and broke bread from house to house. They ate their food with a joyful and humble attitude, 47 praising God and having favor with all the people. And every day the Lord added to them those who were being saved.*[37]

What were those designs for the church? They were:

1. Devotion
2. Study of the Word of God
3. Breaking of Bread Together
4. Preaching
5. Prayer
6. Fasting
7. Giving sacrificially
8. Fellowship
9. Disciple Making

---

[37] The Holy Bible: Holman Christian Standard Version. (Nashville: Holman Bible Publishers, 2009), Acts 2:42–47.

10. Acts of Service

In the Book of Revelation John states to the Sardis church: *"I know all the things you do, and that you have a reputation for being alive, but you are dead."*

But we must look inward and consider our own congregation. We must examine ourselves and see what areas we need to address in order to bring our church back towards revitalization and renewal. We must repair what is fractured.

II. We Must Remove What Does Not Fit (vs. 4-5).

Notice that Hezekiah immediately called together all of the Levites:

> *4 "Then he brought in the priests and Levites and gathered them in the eastern public square. 5 He said to them, "Hear me, Levites. Consecrate yourselves now and consecrate the temple of Yahweh, the God of your ancestors. Remove everything impure from the holy place."*

He commanded them to sanctify themselves so they could clean up the house of God. As he charged them to sanctify the house of God, he reminded them that the pitiful plight of Judah was caused by unfaithfulness to God. The Levites were quick to respond to the will of the king in this matter. They cleansed the house of God. Then they sanctified and purified themselves from their ceremonial uncleanness. After this, they proceeded to ceremonially sanctify the Temple. He said to them to remove what does not fit and that which does not fit in any church today is the filthiness of the world, which has defiled the church of the Lord. Even today there are things in which we allow to invade our churches all across this land and like the young king we also must remove the world's sin as it invades our churches. When the priests and the Levites reported to the king that they had finished, he called the rulers of the city to the house of God. At this time, he reinstituted the sacrifices and all of the rituals that went with them. Then he invited the whole congregation to bring their sacrifices to the house of God. So great was the response that there were not enough priests to take care of the sacrificial offerings. Therefore the Levites had to help them.

Where Ahaz had formerly ignited the fury of The Lord, when Hezekiah ascended to the throne he took the proper actions in order to purge the temple of the things that did not fit in a church, which is holy and focused on the Lord. When there are things in the church that do not belong, the only answer is to understand that we must remove what does not fit.

In the New Testament we see an example of Jesus removing that, which does not fit within the house of God. In Matthew 21:12-13, as Jesus entered the Temple of God he said:

> *"The Scriptures declare, 'My Temple will be called a house of prayer,' but you have turned it into a den of thieves!"*

If you want to see your church revitalized and renewed, the Lord's house must return to a place of worship focused on God and not on those who believe the church should be focused on them. The Lord Jesus is not pleased today when His people gather together and His Father is not glorified! There are some churches today that are nothing more than big businesses and their goal is profit. There are some churches today and they are nothing more than the local civic center. These churches are always busy, but they are busy doing the wrong things and the problem is in the fact that you cannot find discipleship, evangelism or the Gospel!

Not only are there some bad churches which are a front to the Lord, there are some churches which we would perhaps call good because godly people attend there. Yet they have allowed the world's ways to creep in. False teachings have been allowed to enter the church. Worldliness has been allowed to enter the church. Liberalism and legalism has been allowed to enter the church. Disunity has been allowed to enter the church. Ones personal program over the Lord's, has been allowed to enter the church. We must remove what does not fit the Lord's ideal in this church or any church. There is no place for anything here, which runs counter to the teaching of the Word of God. We can no longer center our future hope on the things we have always done, but on what the Lord would have us to do today! The process of removing what does not fit starts with all of us and each one of us. Are there things in your life today that need to be removed? Is there an act of sin within our lives that we are not giving over to God and asking for His victory and forgiveness? Like young Hezekiah not only do we need to take a stand against past sins, sometimes we must take a stand against those who would allow sin to run rampant within the church.

In 2 Kings 18:4 it reads that Hezekiah:

"removed the high places, and broke the images, and
cut down the groves, and broke in pieces the brazen
serpent that Moses had made: for unto those days the
children of Israel did burn incense to it: and he called
it Nehushtan (nothing more than brass)."

The brazen serpent that Moses had made was broken into pieces. The people had ignored that God had created it and began to worship it in a pagan manner by burning incense to it. There were some obstacles that Hezekiah encountered that had to be confronted. Listen oh child of God; if the behaviors, habits, and rituals of your fathers come before your devotion to God, then we need to remove what does not fit. Hezekiah ignored the devotion to his father and destroyed the idols that he had set in place.

Will you remove the things that do not belong from your life today? Luke 16:13 says: "No servant can serve two masters: for either he will hate the one and love the other; or else he will hold to the one and despise the other."

We must remove what does not fit and we must follow the steps that Hezekiah outlined for the "Priests and Levites" when he declared:

"sanctify yourselves, and sanctify the house of the
LORD God of your fathers, and carry forth the filthiness out of the holy place."

This process begins with us as individuals. Each one of us within the reception of my voice, must take a long hard look in the mirror and realize that we have a part in revitalizing this dear church. In order to do that, we must:

We Must Repair What Is Fractured and We Must Remove What Does Not Fit. What steps will you take today in individual renewal and spiritual renewal? Turning a church around and getting it back on the road of health is not easy, but we must take those steps to become what God would have us to become. We must do those things that are necessary for us to honor and glorify our Father in Heaven.

Chapter 6

A Focused Church

" *N*or is there salvation in any other, for there is no other name under heaven given among men by which we must be saved."

The Name of Jesus Forbidden

Now when they saw the boldness of Peter and John, and perceived that they were uneducated and untrained men, they marveled. And they realized that they had been with Jesus. And seeing the man who had been healed standing with them, they could say nothing against it. But when they had commanded them to go aside out of the council, they conferred among themselves, saying, "What shall we do to these men? For, indeed, that a notable miracle has been done through them *is* evident to all who dwell in Jerusalem, and we cannot deny *it*. But so that it spreads no further among the people, let us severely threaten them, that from now on they speak to no man in this name." So they called them and commanded them not to speak at all nor teach in the name of Jesus. But Peter and John answered and said to them, "Whether it is right in the sight of God to listen to you more than to God, you judge. For we cannot but speak the things which we have seen and heard." So when they had further threatened them, they let them go, finding no way of punishing them, because of the people, since they all glorified God for what had been done. For the man was over forty years old on whom this miracle of healing had been performed.

Prayer for Boldness

And being let go, they went to their own *companions* and reported all that the chief priests and elders had said to them. So when they heard that, they raised their voice to God with one accord and said: "Lord, You *are* God, who made heaven and earth and the sea, and all that is in them, who by the mouth of Your servant David have said: 'Why did the nations rage, And the people plot vain things? The kings of the earth took their stand, and the rulers were gathered together against the Lord and against His Christ. "For truly against Your holy Servant Jesus, whom You anointed, both Herod and Pontius Pilate, with the Gentiles and the people of Israel, were gathered together to do whatever Your hand and Your purpose determined before to be done. Now, Lord, look on their threats, and grant to Your servants that with all boldness they may speak Your word, by stretching out Your hand to heal, and that signs and wonders may be done through the name of Your holy Servant Jesus." And when they had prayed, the place where they were assembled together was shaken; and they were all filled with the Holy Spirit, and they spoke the word of God with boldness." (Acts 4:12-31 NKJV) [38]

I recently took up photography as a hobby. Little did I know there was so much to learn once I took the camera off automatic. Terms like depth of field, shutter speed, ISO, aperture priority are just a few of the terms I have learned are important to taking better pictures. But the main thing I have learned is the importance of making sure the subject of the photograph is in focus. Every instructor I have set under has reminded me repeatedly that an exceptional photo is one where the viewer's eyes are drawn to an in-focus subject. If the subject is not sharply focused the photograph loses its impact.

---

[38] Scripture quotations are taken from the New King James Version (Nashville, TN: Thomas Nelson Inc., Publishers, 1979, 1980, 1982).

I believe the same is true for the church as well. Often our focus is so blurred we have little if any impact on the world we are trying to reach with the Gospel. One of Satan's primary tools, I believe, is to lead the church to focus on everything, but the important things. If the enemy can get us to distort our purpose and our mission he has won.

Where can you find an example of a focused church? There is none better than the First Century Church. Amidst criticism, threats, and persecution the first century church stayed focused on Christ and His mission. There is no better passage that illustrates this than Acts 4. Peter and John have been arrested for bringing healing to a man outside the Temple (Acts 3). At the same time thousands respond to their message and are saved. When arrested and threatened they continue to proclaim Jesus as the only way. In essence they speak very clearly they have one reason for their existence. It is to bring hope to people who are hopeless. When Peter and John are finally released they return to the church. Rather than complaining about the treatment received at the hands of the officials they gather with Believers and cry out to God for courage to overcome all obstacles in order to carry the Gospel to the world. As a result the church experienced unprecedented growth. They experienced this growth without facilities, organized programs, or favor with city officials.

What was the secret to the first century church? The bottom line is Believers were filled with the Spirit of God and love for Jesus and the people for whom He died. They were unwilling to allow anything to get in the way of the Gospel. They made no excuse for their focus on certain things. The first century church was careful to not allow even the good to stand in the way of the best. That is a lesson we can learn in today's church. There are a lot of good things we can be involved in, but, unfortunately, the good things often become the enemy of the best things. There are certain foundational principles that led the first century church to impact the world the way that it did. I believe as we adopt these principles we can see greater success today. What are they?

The church must focus on truth rather than tradition. The message of the early church was Jesus. (Acts 4:12) "Nor is there salvation in any other, for there is no other name under heaven given among men by which we must be saved." When the disciples made this declaration it was a line in the sand. It wasn't the most popular thing they could have said; in fact it cost them dearly. The entire ministry of the church was based on this declaration. There was no room for compromise when it came to Jesus.

The message has remained unchanged through the centuries. That is the message of the church today. The church is called upon to meet the physical, emotional, and social needs of people, but, primarily, the mission is to point people to the cross of Christ. This is not to say the church is not to meet needs in the community. In fact, I believe, one of the major mistakes many churches make is to disconnect from the community. Jesus taught we are to be concerned with people's needs. Matthew 25: 35-36 says, "for I was hungry and you gave Me food; I was thirsty and you gave Me drink; I was a stranger and you took Me in; I was naked and you clothed Me; I was sick and you visited Me; I was in prison and you came to Me." As the church demonstrates it really cares about people, doors are opened for the Gospel. We just need to be sure we don't neglect to care about a person's spiritual well being as we care about their physical well being.

While the message is paramount we must be very careful not to confuse the message with our methods. Our message is sacred, but our methods are not. People have a tendency to deify methods and programs. Jesus addressed this issue with the Pharisees. "For laying aside the commandment of God, you hold the tradition of men — the washing of pitchers and cups, and many other such things you do. He said to them, "*All too* well you reject the commandment of God, that you may keep your tradition" (Mark 7:8-9).

One of the easiest things to do in church life is to start something. One of the most difficult is to end what has been started. Why do we do much of what we do in church? The answer is simple; because we have always done these things. There are programs we continue long after their effectiveness has diminished or completely run its course. Most of these efforts were started because they helped the church carry out its mission. They are continued past their effectiveness, because they become entrenched as traditions. Unfortunately when that happens they impede the mission of the church rather than promote it. We should be defined not only by what we start doing, but also by what we stop doing.

94

Most of the church problems I have seen have been over tradition not Biblical principles. Try moving someone's classroom to a new location, or let a guest sit in a church member's regular seat in the Sanctuary. There are times when the church is more committed to an outdated set of By-laws than the Bible. I heard of one church that fired its pastor over a public safety day. The church honored firemen, police, and emergency medical personnel. Unfortunately the deacons hadn't voted on it. In this church it was a tradition that the deacons voted on everything. Since when do we have to vote on showing love to people? We would do well to heed the warning we read from Mark 7: 8-9. Let us not be guilty of rejecting God's commandments for our traditions. Remember, Jesus summarized the commandments this way. "...You shall love the Lord your God with all your heart, with all your soul, and with all your mind. This is *the* first and great commandment. And *the* second *is* like it: 'You shall love your neighbor as yourself'. On these two commandments hang all the Law and the Prophets." (Matthew 22:37-40) I believe it is tradition that is killing many of our churches. We can become so structured we structure Jesus right out of the church. If we would simply focus on the two greatest commandments and do everything we could do to live them out personally and in the church, I believe ministry would thrive.

The church must focus on challenges as opportunities rather than obstacles. The first century church faced many challenges that could, humanly speaking, be considered almost insurmountable obstacles to success. This church had no property, few possessions, and a lack of popularity with the religious establishment and only the threat of imprisonment or worse to those who joined. Yet, they experienced phenomenal growth. This is the setting of Acts 4. Conditions were less than favorable. The choice was simple. Give up or go on in the power of the Holy Spirit. They chose, thankfully for us today, to go on rather than give in or give up.

We are often limited in the church by our focus. It is easy to dwell on what we don't have to the point of forgetting what is available to us. If only...becomes a crippling attitude in the church. If only we had more money, a better location, better people, etc we could be stronger. While those things are helpful there is something we have that trumps all of them. We have the power of the Holy Spirit available to us to carry out the work Christ gives to us.

Early in my ministry I attended a conference where an "expert" was coming from another state to speak on church growth. I attended with great expectancy and with pen and paper in hand. I will never forget how he started out. He said "In order to see the church grow and have impact there are some things you must have." Ok, I was ready to list those magic bullets. He started by saying "You must have a great location." My anticipation turned to a little disappointment pretty quickly. You see, the church I pastored was located in a small town. In fact, not many people even knew the town existed. I wasn't too disappointed, because my reasoning was, "I can overcome that if the rest of his list is workable." He proceeded to say, "Next, you need a strong budget." That is when I began to experience a sick feeling in the pit of my stomach. Our annual church budget was $25,000. That was everything and I do mean everything. That included evangelism, missions, Sunday School, the power bill, and the pastor's salary. If that wasn't enough, his next statement really sent me into the depths of despair. "You must have great facilities." I was sunk. Our Sanctuary was nice but small, but we had only one very small, older classroom building. I will never forget how I felt. This was the expert. He must know what he is talking about. I have never felt so low in ministry. But, he wasn't done. He concluded his remarks by saying, "You must be a dynamic speaker." Ok, that was the nail in the coffin. There was no way the church I pastored could ever grow. Above all we didn't have the dynamic speaker. I was the speaker, and I was far from dynamic. I left this conference totally defeated. I will never forget driving up to my small church, in our small community that day. I walked into the church and fell on the altar. I said to God, "Ok, God, I now know it can't happen through me, and it can't happen here. I have none of the things available to me the expert says I must have." That is when God spoke. Mind you, not in an audible voice; no, it was much louder than that. What He said to me in my heart that day has shaped my ministry. "You don't have the facility, the location, the budget, or the dynamic speaker, but there are some things you do have. You have Me, and you have the power of my Holy Spirit. You also have people around your church who don't know me, so stop your pity party and allow Me to show you how you can mobilize your small church to get outside the walls, through the power of a huge God, and really impact a community.

The First century church teaches us how to focus on what is available to us rather than what we lack. When, in Acts 3, Peter and John approached the crippled man he asked for money. Peter said, "...Silver and gold I do not have, but what I do have I give you: In the name of Jesus Christ of Nazareth, rise up and walk." (Acts 3:6) In photography I have learned about focus points. Where you place the focus point is where you will have sharpness. As the church we have to decide where our focus point is going to be. Will it be on what we lack, or will it be on "the name of Jesus Christ of Nazareth," in whom there is great power?

How did the early church tap into the power of God? How did they get their focus on the right things? It is simple, every challenge the church faced was handled in a prayer meeting. There was a deep dependency on the resources and power of God. How has that changed today? I believe one of our major problems in the church is we attempt to handle in a business meeting what we should first address in a prayer meeting. When our dependency is on programs, the opinions of man, and procedures we get far less than what we get when we depend on God! How did E.M. Bounds, the great writer on prayer put it? "Prayer succeeds when all else fails."[39] It was also Bounds who said, "The story of every great Christian achievement is the history of answered prayer."[40]

Look at the difference. The early church was characterized by power and boldness. The average church today is characterized by paralysis and bureaucracy.

The early church was also characterized by perseverance. The word "quit" was not part of their vocabulary. No matter the obstacle this church moved on. Look at Acts 4. "So they called them and commanded them not to speak at all nor teach in the name of Jesus. But Peter and John answered and said to them, "Whether it is right

---

[39] E.M. Bounds, *Purpose in Prayer* (New York, NY: Fleming H. Revell Company, 1920).

[40] Ibid.

in the sight of God to listen to you more than to God, you judge. For we cannot but speak the things which we have seen and heard" (Acts 4:18-20).

We need an old fashioned dose of perseverance in today's church. The attitude of much of society today is, "If you don't first succeed, quit." This attitude has permeated the church. When I was young I played little league baseball. Like today, sponsors could advertise on the outfield fence. One space was reserved for a non-sponsored sign. I will never forget how this sign read. The words were simple, but have impacted me greatly. They were, "Be a hitter, not a quitter." Churches very seldom change and grow without struggle. It is easy to give up, accept status quo, and to retreat to tradition rather than battle the enemy for the souls of men and women. We need the church to adopt the "hitter" rather than "quitter" mentality. We need the church today to be modeled after the church in Acts.

The church must focus on people rather than programs. The church in Acts was focused on people. Acts 4:31 "And when they had prayed, the place where they were assembled together was shaken; and they were all filled with the Holy Spirit, and they spoke the word of God with boldness." These Believers didn't wait for people to come to them. They reached out in boldness. The day has passed, if it ever really existed, when we can simply open the doors of the church, establish our programs, and hope to see people who need what the church has to offer to just wander in. That will happen on occasion, but not very often. The problem lies when we structure our ministry around our programs rather than around people and their needs. If we don't reach out to people, connect with them, and show them the love of Christ, we cannot expect them to participate in our churches. It is beyond question that most people who attend a church for the first time do not attend because of the worship service or programs. They attend, because someone has personally invited them. This is especially true for the person who has no connection to church. They have no clue what goes on inside the doors of the church. It is friendship that brings them. One Sunday I said to our congregation that we are mistaken if we think the people who pass our church even have us on their radar. The next Sunday, following my weekly routine, I stopped at the convenience store across from the church to grab a big cup of coffee. My belief is coffee and the Holy Spirit make for a great early service. While filling my coffee cup I noticed a family of four come through the door. They were dressed for a soccer game. Undoubtedly they had gotten up late, because they were arguing. Dad was trying to hurry everyone along, and the rest of the family wasn't happy about it. As they left the store I watched them get into their car and drive away. They drove right past our new LED lighted sign and our church campus without ever once looking over at our nice church buildings. It was as if God said to me, "See, people really do not have you on their radar." Truthfully, I can't find in the Scripture where we should be on the radar of the un-churched. I can find many Scriptures that tell us the un-churched should be on our radar.

When they do come, if there is not a spirit of friendliness and acceptance, they are sure not to return. The large majority of people who attend a church for the first time have decided long before the sermon whether they are going to return. The decision is made based on how people treat them when they arrive and when they enter the building. "Why do most people not attend church? Because they have been to church?" I know it's a cliché, but it is very convicting. Several years ago a man visited our church for the first time. The building was crowded, and he turned to leave. One of our men who volunteered to greet people in the parking lot noticed him. He asked if he could be of help. The guest explained this was his first visit to the church and didn't really know where to sit. This perceptive volunteer asked him where he worked. When he told him General Motors he asked if he knew certain men who attended the church who also worked for this company. The gentleman who was visiting eyes brightened. He said, "I do." Our volunteer helped him find one of his co-workers with whom he sat that Sunday. It wasn't long before our guest gave his life to Christ. One day he dropped by my office. He burst in and said, "I want to do something in the church." It is not everyday that happens, so I was extremely excited. "What would you like to do? I asked." He quickly said, "I don't know what you call it, but I want to do what the man was doing in the parking lot when I came to church my first Sunday." He then said, "I am going to heaven because of that man!" Never underestimate the power of friendliness.

Question, are we focused? If so, are we focused on the right things? What do we need to start doing, and just as importantly, what do we need to stop doing? Are we focused primarily on what we lack or what we have in Christ? Are we focused on our programs that may or may not be effective, or are we focused on the people for whom Christ came and died? What is our model for doing church? Is it the church in Acts? It is never too late to pray and see what God can do. Remember as we have already said, in the words of E.M. Bounds, "The story of every great Christian achievement is the history of answered prayer."

Chapter 7

The Need for Repentance in Church Renewal

Hosea 14:1-9

*T*his is the end of Hosea's prophecy. It begins with a call to repentance. It begins with prayer. The people of Israel needed to seek God's grace and forgiveness, renew their alliance to Him by renouncing foreign alliances, and their own reliance in their military and their self-made images. As you move your local church forward in the work of Church Revitalization, you will eventually confront the need for the church to corporately and for individuals singularly, to come to repentance of past sins if the church is to get growing again! For most of us that is a huge ouch. Calling the church to repentance is one thing, but admitting that I might need to personally confess and repent of past sins is another. Yet the call to repentance for a church and its people is vital to its turnaround efforts. That is a big OUCH for most of us as believers isn't it?

Look with me at Hosea 14:1-9 as we consider the need for repentance in church renewal:

> Israel, return to Yahweh your God, for you have stumbled in your sin. 2 Take words of repentance with you and return to the LORD. Say to Him: "Forgive all our sins and accept what is good, so that we may repay

You with praise from our lips. 3 Assyria will not save us, we will not ride on horses, and we will no longer proclaim, 'Our gods!' to the work of our hands. For the fatherless receives compassion in You." 4 I will heal their apostasy; I will freely love them, for My anger will have turned from him. 5 I will be like the dew to Israel; he will blossom like the lily and take root like the cedars of Lebanon. 6 His new branches will spread, and his splendor will be like the olive tree, his fragrance, like the forest of Lebanon. 7 The people will return and live beneath his shade. They will grow grain and blossom like the vine. His renown will be like the wine of Lebanon. 8 Ephraim, why should I have anything more to do with idols? It is I who answer and watch over him. I am like a flourishing pine tree; your fruit comes from Me.[41]

There is a great story about Thomas Jefferson founder of the University of Virginia. One day, the misbehavior of students led to a riot in which professors who tried to restore order were being attacked. The following day a meeting was held between the university's board, of which Jefferson was a member, and some of those defiant students. Thomas Jefferson began by saying, "This is one of the most painful events of my life," suddenly he was overcome by emotion, and burst into tears. Another board member asked the protestors to come forward and give their names. Nearly every one did. Later, one of the activists said, "It was not Mr. Jefferson's words, but his tears."[42]

Just like the dissident student was moved by Jefferson's brokenness, so is God moved by our brokenness. When we are truly broken and sorry for our sins, this leads to repentance. As you move forward in the work of Church Revitalization, you will eventually confront the need for the church to corporately and for individuals singularly,

---

[41] The Holy Bible: Holman Christian Standard Version. (Nashville: Holman Bible Publishers, 2009), Hosea 14:1–8.

[42] Source Unknown

to come to repentance of past sins if the church is to get growing again. Now that is a big O.U.C.H. for most of us as believers isn't it? Let's look at it from God's eyes today:

- Offering
- Undivided
- Commitment to the Holy One

When calling any church to repentance, it is crucial that as the leader, we draw a line in the sand starting point and set a moving forward from here launching date. I experienced this in a former church I came to revitalize and restart. Things had been wrong in the past and had gone terribly wrong with the previous leadership. My first sermon to these wonderful people was dealing with a pulpit of integrity! That day I asked the amazing members of the church to stand with me (literally) and draw a line in the sand that regardless of what had happened in the past, on that day forward, we would commit to being the type of church and the type of people who desired to see God's hand come upon us once again. That day we set a moving forward from here date and the church began dealing with individual and corporate repentance!

So here is the OUCH question I would like to ask for your consideration: are you or this dear church, which Christ Jesus died for, covering up past sins? That is a startling and challenging question today, yet it is the beginning point, the middle point, and the final point in seeing the hand of God return to bless this church. I believe it is time to begin "fessing" up by calling this church to personal and corporate church repentance. It is a call to holiness for me as your leader and a call for you as children of God. When we consider the sin that this passage speaks of today, we see that sin will always result in one of two responses: we either cover it up or confess to the Lord our God. Our church's future and our future as individuals depend on our response to Gods invitation of confession.

If we should investigate and contemplate the church's past, and we should, we will soon realize that some things in it are not worth celebrating. In fact there are things in our history that have caused us to become a declining church. May I remind you today what most of us already know and that is, something that was wrong in the church in the past, is always dead wrong still unless it is confessed. This means the church is in need of repentance now. We are here today at a crossroads of opportunity for God to do a new thing. Repentance is a critical part of God's forgiveness and advancement towards a renewed church.

This is not as depressing as it sounds because here it represents an opportunity for God to do a new thing. As the prophet Hosea reminds us if we are going to see the hand of God return to our church there is:

1. The Necessity of Honest Repentance – vs. 1

Hosea cries out to his countrymen:

> *"Israel, return to Yahweh your God, for you have stumbled in your sin."*

Here is a wonderful gift from God as he gives the children of Israel a call to repentance. This same call is available to each and every one of us today. God does not reluctantly offer forgiveness to sinful people. The Book of Hosea concludes with a final call for repentance. The prophet paints a beautiful picture of what God would do for his penitent people. The Hebrew uses a preposition which means more than merely turning to Yahweh. It means complete conversion. The salvation of God must be preceded by genuine repentance. *"For you have stumbled in your sin."* Sin is represented as a false step. The words could be describing something which had happened already.

There is a difference between forgiving sin and overlooking it. The Lord wants to do more than forgive the sin; He wants to transform the sinner. To automatically forgive sin with no requirements involved would be to excuse it. This within itself would be an encouragement to sin. God's condition for forgiveness is true repentance. What we have here in these precious verses are directions for repentance and what to do in order to repent and receive forgiveness. Hosea even gives us what to say so we can be sure we are really coming to God in a spirit of confession seeking forgiveness.

There is a story told about a Sunday School teacher who once asked a class what was meant by the word "repentance." A little boy put up his hand and said, "It is being sorry for your sins." A little girl also raised her hand and said, "It is being sorry enough to quit."

Though His people may turn away from Him, God will not forsake them, even though He disciplines them, for He is true to His covenant and His promises.

"If we are faithless, He remains faithful; He cannot deny Himself" (2 Tim. 2:13, NKJV).

God pleads with His people to come back to Him, to return to Him and to forsake the sins that were causing their downfall. The Lord has made a great work in providing for us the ability to repent of our sin. Sin is a fall and the only way those that have fallen by sin to get up again is by repentance.

2. The Nature of Honest Repentance – vs. 2.

"Take words of repentance with you and return to the LORD. Say to Him: Forgive all our sins and accept what is good, so that we may repay You with praise from our lips."

In this verse the Lord God is inviting them to return to Him. Yet He asks for a price to be paid. They must confess their sins. Eugene Peterson says this, "No judgment is inevitable. Repentance can radically change the course of events. The moment we turn away from all god-substitutes—become an 'orphan' to the world—and return to God, new life begins to flow."[43] In this verse and the next we see a prayer of repentance for the things, which have been done. The

---

[43] Praying with the Prophets September 30.

phrase *"Take words of repentance with"* implies speaking words of sincere confession, repentance, and faith. Douglas Stuart in the Word Bible Commentary says that: "The invitation to return is thus a real word of hope for the nation as a continuum, though not a prediction of blessing for the same generation who first heard these words from Hosea's lips."[44]

For those who come after and will be the remnant seeking repentance and forgiveness, Hosea provides a sample vow of atonement for repentance. I do not believe what we have here is an exact blueprint, but more of a synopsis of their plea. What I want you to see here is in Exodus 23:15 and Exodus 34:20 the Israelites were instructed to bring a sacrifice offering to assure ones vow. Yet here Hosea the prophet does not tell them to take a sacrifice to the Lord. I think the reason for that is any sacrifice we bring to the Lord is totally worthless without obedience. Instead we are to take words of confession which will be supported by true actions that will satisfy that promise. God is happy to give them the words for their speech and to teach them what they shall say.

Here Hosea was giving the people the sample vow of atonement for repentance not the exact words to say. The nature of these honest words for repentance is threefold. He says:

> *"Take words of repentance with you and return to the LORD"* which deals with repentance.

> *"Say to Him: "Forgive all our sins and accept what is good"* which allows for confession.
> "So that we may repay You with praise from our lips" which demonstrates a renewed commitment.

So too should each one of us repent of and confess our sins, confess Jesus as our Savior by grace through faith, and commit yourself to Him as Lord with the pledge to share our experience with other lost people. The sacrifice which God desires most is the

---

[44] Douglas Stuart, Hosea–Jonah, vol. 31, Word Biblical Commentary (Dallas: Word, Incorporated, 2002), 212–218.

acknowledgement of sin. We see the necessity of honest repentance. We see the nature of honest repentance.

3. The Renunciation in Honest Repentance – vs. 3.

"Assyria will not save us, we will not ride on horses, and we will no longer proclaim, 'Our gods!' to the work of our hands. For the fatherless receives compassion in You."

Turning to God in honest repentance requires renunciation of the world, of its power, and its false gods. Thus the repentant must say first: *""Assyria will not save us."* They will no longer rely on political alliance to solve their problems. In Hosea's time, Israel had been tempted to turn to Assyria for help. The fact of the matter is that Assyria proved to be Israel's downfall. Second, they must declare: *"we will not ride on horses."* They would no longer trust in military supremacy. The reference may be to Egypt, the country which supplied Palestine with horses. Third, the contrite one must denounce idolatry: *"we will no longer proclaim, 'Our gods!' to the work of our hands."* Foreign gods as well as foreign alliances are renounced by those who wish to get right with God. Fourth, the repentant must recognize that Yahweh is a merciful Father: *"For the fatherless receives compassion in You."* Because of His compassion, the repenting can be assured of forgiveness.

We see the necessity of honest repentance. We see the nature of honest repentance. We see the renunciation in honest repentance.

4. God's Notice for Honest Repentance – vs. 4.

"I will heal their apostasy; I will freely love them, for My anger will have turned from him."

The Lord's notice for honest repentance is to respond in mercy. Sin not only needs to be forgiven, but sin needs to be healed. Sin can become an addiction and not only is it a violation of God's Word; it leaves a scar on each of us. No matter what the era of human history,

God responds to the repentant heart. Scripture says *that if we confess our sins, God is faithful and just and will forgive us our sins.* So we are to confess our sins to God. He will restore us. God restores the penitent to spiritual health and heals their backsliding.[45] But we are also to confess our sins to one another. Scripture tells us to do that, too! The thought of confessing may make us uncomfortable, but it's a vital-part of changing directions and getting on the right road with God. There is a divine response to honest repentance. Individual repentance removes God's wrath.

When an individual comes down with an infection, it is usually the effect of a progression that has been operating in the body for weeks. First an infection gets into the system and begins to grow. The individual experiences exhaustion and loss of appetite, then weakness, and then the illness occurs. In like manner when sin gets into the inner person and is not dealt with, it acts like an insidious infection: it grows quietly; it brings loss of spiritual appetite; it creates weariness and weakness; then comes the collapse.

We see the necessity of honest repentance. We see the nature of honest repentance.

We see the renunciation in honest repentance. We see God's notice for honest repentance.

5. The New Life of Honest Repentance vs. 5 -8.

> *"I will be like the dew to Israel; he will blossom like the lily and take root like the cedars of Lebanon. 6 His new branches will spread, and his splendor will be like the olive tree, his fragrance, like the forest of Lebanon. 7 The people will return and live beneath his shade. They will grow grain and blossom like the vine. His renown will be like the wine of Lebanon. 8 Ephraim, why should I have anything more to do with idols? It is I who answer and watch over him. I am like a flourishing pine tree; your fruit comes from Me."*

---

[45] C.f. Jeremiah 14:7.

108

The Lord will revive us. There is a long-range result of repentance. Hosea pictures the restoration of the repentant as the emergence of new life in a dry field on which the refreshing dew has fallen. Dew is a emblem of the Holy Spirit:

Silent in its approach
Saturating in its interaction
Refreshing in its ministry
Always rich in its substance
Always falls most in the lowliest of dwellings

In the summer and early autumn in the Holy Land, the dew is very heavy and greatly appreciated.[46] That's what the word "revive" means: to bring new life. The rich vegetation appears, producing beauty and fragrance where once the farmer saw only ugliness and emptiness. The fallow ground becomes a fruitful garden! A revived and repentance Israel would have deep and broad roots like the cedars of Lebanon, And they would be as beautiful as the olive tree. The widespread branches symbolize abiding prosperity. And they are known for their smell or sweet fragrance.

6. The News of Honest Repentance–vs. 9.

> *"Who wise, and he shall understand these? Prudent, and he shall know them? For the ways of the LORD right, and the just shall walk in them: but the transgressors shall fall therein."*

The Book of Hosea closes with a warning. The message of the entire book is summed up in this concluding verse. We learn that there are two classes of people in God's economy. There are the *"just"* and the *"transgressors"*. This has always been the case since Adam fell and sin entered into the world. We learn that *"the just"* walk in the ways of the Lord, whereas *"the transgressors"* walk in their own

---

[46] C.f. Psalm 133:3; Isaiah 18:4.

ways. They are different in the way they walk, the path in which they walk, the one for whom they walk and the destiny to which they walk. The closing verse presents us with only two alternatives:

We can rebel against the Lord and continue to stumble, or
We can return to the Lord and walk securely in His ways.

The first choice is foolish; the second choice is wise. We learn that God's way is right and man's way is wrong.

"I have set before you life and death, blessing and cursing; therefore, choose life" (Deut. 30:19).

Nothing can quench God's love for His people. Like a marriage spouse, God is intensely involved in their lives and is pained by their rebellion and unfaithfulness. God demands love and loyalty from His own. Often God's people then and now have failed to demonstrate wholehearted love for Him. But God stands ready to forgive and restore those who turn to Him in repentance. Please do not miss the personal message here: backsliders may return to the Lord, experience His forgiveness, and be restored to the place of blessing and usefulness. Approximately 2,800 years separate us from Hosea's day. His prophecy was needed then. It is needed today. God still responds to people who genuinely repent of their sins by forgiving them and giving them eternal life. Repentance is the turning point, when our relationship with God is restored to solid footing and we can move forward in a loving relationship with the Lord.

All this dialogue about repentance stems from two very deep realities. The first reality is that each one of us is made for a loving and growing relationship with God. The second reality is that because of our sin, we are far from it!

It may be that God has been withholding his blessing because the body has not repented and when it does repent, it will open the floodgates and pour out His grace an unprecedented measure. As we have noted we can respond in one of two ways when we have sin. We can cover up or we can fess up! The choice to disobey God is ours and ours alone. We have only ourselves to blame and the same is true of any church, which has failed God in the past. Therefore if we are to experience consecration, we must begin with personal ownership and agreement with God that we are the ones responsible for the sins that we have committed!

Hosea 11:4 is a word of action for us today:

> *"I will heal their apostasy; I will freely love them, for My anger will have turned from him."*

Dear believer, it is time to reclaim verse four for yourself and experience the healing of sins forgiven.

We see the necessity of honest repentance. We see the nature of honest repentance.

We see the renunciation in honest repentance. We see God's notice for honest repentance. We see the new life of honest repentance. We see the news of honest repentance.

Chapter 8

A Primary Task

Psalm 126:6

"He who continually goes forth weeping, Bearing seed for sowing, Shall doubtless come again with rejoicing, Bringing his sheaves with him."
(Psalm 126:6 NKJV)[47]

𝓜ax Lucado in, *On the Anvil* [48] gives one of the best illustrations of the church I have seen. He calls it "The Movement that was Doomed to Fail." He starts by saying the people were few. "Only 120 men and women who were poor, not well educated, and immersed in a society that was corrupt were used of God to begin a movement called the church. Not only did the church begin with a small number of common people, but also their strategy was disastrous. No headquarters, no professional plan, and no real understanding of their mission." These are not the makings of a successful movement in anyone's book.

---

[47] Scripture quotations are taken from the New King James Version (Nashville, TN: Thomas Nelson Inc., Publishers, 1979,1980, 1982).

[48] Max Lucado, *On the Anvil* (Carol Stream, IL: Tyndale House Publishers, Inc., 2008).

Yet, as Lucado states, "the movement didn't fail." It succeeded, as he points out, because: It was born of God, not man. It was bathed in the power of the Holy Spirit. It was built upon prayer. It was bold to carry out its mission."

If a church is to succeed today, it will be for the same reasons. Our security is in God, not man. Our strength is in the Holy Spirit. Our stability is in prayer. Our success is found in carrying out the mission God has assigned to us.

Our success depends on our focus. We must focus on our mission rather than focus on all that attempts to distract us from that mission. What is that mission? It is very simply put, to take the Gospel of Christ to the world. If you get right down to it there is no more important reason for our existence. Jesus, in Matthew 28:19-20 made the mission very clear. "And Jesus came and spoke to them, saying, "All authority has been given to Me in heaven and on earth. Go therefore and make disciples of all the nations, baptizing them in the name of the Father and of the Son and of the Holy Spirit, teaching them to observe all things that I have commanded you; and lo, I am with you always, *even* to the end of the age." (Matthew 28:18-20) Amen.

In Acts 1:8 He defined our mission field. "But you shall receive power when the Holy Spirit has come upon you; and you shall be witnesses to Me in Jerusalem, and in all Judea and Samaria, and to the end of the earth."

We cannot be content to do business as usual if we are going to carry out the assignment God has given us. We cannot ignore what God has told us; we must be willing to obey His commands. Psalm 126:6 offers us a challenge, if obeyed, will lead to success in our mission. It is a personal challenge to us as individual Christians and a corporate challenge to the church. This great verse begins with a challenge and concludes with a promise.

We must be a **body committed to the challenge.** The picture in the verse is very clear. It is the picture of a farmer carrying his bag of seed into the field and spreading them. Farming is hard work, but the process is simple. In order for there to be a harvest there must be someone who is willing to sow seed. I grew up in South Georgia where farming is a primary occupation. In fact, while in high school, I spent several summers working on a farm. It has never ceased to amaze me how a small seed placed in the ground and cultivated could produce the way that it does. This is the picture we find in Psalm 126:6. Jesus used the same terminology in the New Testament. The analogy of the farmer is the Believer and the church carrying Christ's message to the world.

The principle is challenging. The primary task of the church is to take the Gospel to the world. This challenge is to every individual, every church, and every organization within the church. Nothing equals the importance of carrying Christ's message of life and hope to the world.

The word "forth" literally is *to go to and fro continually*. Not merely in a period of revival, or church on Sunday, or on a given night. Continuously we are to be planting seeds of the Gospel. Where we work, in our neighborhoods, at school, wherever we are we are to look for opportunities to engage people with the Gospel. The problem is the longer we are saved the fewer numbers of people we know who are not followers of Christ. As Christians our connections with those who don't know Christ seem to diminish unless we intentionally find ways to build relationships with people outside our circle of friends. What would happen if every committed follower of Christ in the church made an intentional effort to get to know, to pray for, to care for and to share Christ with people who are outside the church? This will not happen until, something else this verse talks about, takes place.

We must **have a burden that is compelling.** "He who goes forth weeping..." What has happened to a burden for souls? The kind of burden Paul had when he said, "I tell the truth in Christ, I am not lying, my conscience also bearing me witness in the Holy Spirit, that I have great sorrow and continual grief in my heart. For I could wish that I myself were accursed from Christ for my brethren, my countrymen according to the flesh," (Romans 9:1-3). Paul was deeply burdened due to the lostness of his fellow countrymen. When is the last time the church wept over lostness? When have you last seen people kneeling at the altar of the church crying out to God for family and friends to be saved? Where there is no burden to compel us, there will be little witness.

We must ask God for a burden because of the pain of lostness. There is much brokenness in our world today. People are hurting, lonely and broken. You only have to scan any media outlet to see the results of brokenness in our world today. Jesus said in (Luke 4:18) "The Spirit of the Lord is upon Me, Because He has anointed Me to preach the gospel to the poor; He has sent Me to heal the brokenhearted, to proclaim liberty to the captives and recovery of sight to the blind, to set at liberty those who are oppressed." It is easy to come into the church, close the doors, sing our songs, listen to sermons and shut out the brokenness of the world. We leave feeling good because we have been to church; yet on the way home we drive by countless hurting people without even seeing their brokenness. We talk a lot about church revitalization. A revitalized church is one that sees brokenness and is burdened to do something about it. It is also true that a real burden for people can lead to revitalization of the church.

We must be burdened because of the penalty of lostness. Do we really believe a person who dies without Christ spends eternity separated from God in a literal Hell? I think William Booth said it well. "The chief danger that confronts the coming century will be religion without the Holy Ghost, Christianity without Christ, forgiveness without repentance, salvation without regeneration, politics without God, and heaven without hell."[49]

We must be compelled by a burden people are searching for something to fill the emptiness in their lives. Not only does eternal life mean heaven, it also means a person can live a fulfilled life now. In (John 10:10) Jesus said, "The thief does not come except to steal, and to kill, and to destroy. I have come that they may have life, and that they may have it more abundantly." No one or nothing gives meaning like Jesus. I believe people are more open to the Gospel than ever. Never has a generation had so much yet, experienced such emptiness as our generation. Technology and affluence have taken us to a new high, but left us with the same longing for something that satisfies. If the church will ask God for a burden that leads to relevance and boldness, I believe we will see a harvest. To be relevant we must realize that programs and methods that worked ten years

---

[49] www.goodreads.com/quotes (Goodreads Inc., 2014).

ago may not work today. We must be willing to change our methods while retaining the message that is relevant to all generations. Never has the church been busier and with less results. Could it be that busyness has replaced a true burden? If we really are burdened that people know Christ, we will be willing do whatever it takes to get this message of hope to them.

Our burden must lead to a **belief we cherish**. We must believe the basis for our mission is the Word of God. The seed is His written word revealing the Living Word Jesus Christ. In this age of relativism we have one absolute. It is the Word of God. We have an unchanging Scripture that presents to us an all-powerful Savior. We must be relevant in our methods, but we must never change our message. The hope of the world is still Jesus Christ. As we read the Scripture and accept it as God's inerrant word, we are given the mission and mandate we need to reach our world. We must take His written word seriously if we are to boldly share the living Word. A great example of this is found in two individuals, Billy Graham and Chuck Templeton. The two were Youth for Christ colleagues. Both had strong pulpits. Some say Templeton was considered the one with the most potential. A Youth for Christ veteran looking back on those early days of ministry said, "This boy Charlie Templeton could really preach." Then things changed. Templeton came out of seminary armed with newly acquired weapons of historical and literary criticism of the Bible. It is told that Graham and Templeton would meet periodically to talk about these things. During one of those conversations Graham said, 'Chuck, look, I haven't a good enough mind to settle these questions. I don't have the time, the inclination, or the set of mind to pursue them. I have found that if I say, The Bible says and God says I get results.' Templeton could not make such surrender. Templeton left the ministry and pursued various things. On the other hand Graham's commitment to the Word 'gave power and authority' to his preaching." Thousands upon thousands have come to Christ as a result of his ministry. I believe as we take the written word and through it deliver the Living Word, we will see people experience the life changing power of Christ.

We must behave our belief. As evangelicals we pride ourselves in saying "we are people of the Book." It is not enough to say we believe the Bible, yet not practice the Bible. (James 1: 22-25) says, "But be doers of the word, and not hearers only, deceiving yourselves. For if anyone is a hearer of the word and not a doer, he is like a man observing his natural face in a mirror; for he observes himself, goes away, and immediately forgets what kind of man he was. But he who looks into the perfect law of liberty and continues *in it,* and is not a forgetful hearer, but a doer of the work, this one will be blessed in what he does." How can we say we cherish the Bible, yet not be burdened to reach people? When it comes to the church the Bible says there are several things that mark a New Testament Church. They are: A commitment to Evangelism, unity, discipleship, prayer, and generosity. Do we truly practice these things? Ask yourself, "What are the core values of my church?" Be careful. I am not speaking of values we are supposed to name. I mean values that are actually practiced. Do we really do everything we can to evangelize the lost? Do we really practice generosity? According to George Barna, "Among born again Christians, which includes both evangelicals and non-evangelicals, 12% tithed in 2012,"[50] which is on par with the average for the past decade. Do we really seek unity based on the mission of the church rather than my preferences as a church member?

A more pointed question is this? Do we behave like Jesus? A Barna study was done in 2013 that addressed this issue. Twenty "agree or disagree" questions based on attitudes and actions encapsulating the actions and attitudes of Jesus were asked. The findings were as follows: "Looking at America's evangelical community—a group defined by Barna Group based on its theological beliefs and commitments, not self-identification with the terms "evangelical"—38% qualify as neither Christ-like in action nor attitude, according to their responses to these 20 questions. About one-quarter (23%) of evangelicals are characterized by having Jesus-like actions and attitudes, which was higher than the norm. About half were a mixture of Christ-like actions and Pharisaical attitudes (25%) or vice versa (15%)."[51]

---

[50] George Barna, www.barna.org (Ventura, CA: The Barna Group is an evangelical Christian polling firm. 2012).

[51] George Barna, www.barna.org (Ventura, CA: The Barna Group is an evangelical Christian polling firm. 2013) .

I believe if we really want people to desire our Jesus we as Christ followers need to look more like Him.

When we are committed to the mission, have a real burden for people and deliver the message of Christ both in word and lifestyle, I believe we will discover **a blessing to be celebrated**. "Shall doubtless come again with rejoicing, bringing His sheaves with him." It is the positive side of "reaping what we sow." (Psalm 126:6) Why is the church stagnant? Why are fewer people coming to Christ? I believe it is because fewer people are actually sharing Him. The church is focused on everything but the main thing. What will bring more joy into the church? I believe it is more people coming to Christ.

People love it when babies are born. There is great joy when a new life comes into the world. You can always tell where the new babies are in church. There will always be a crowd in that area. Proud parents and grandparents can't wait to show off the precious little life God has brought into their world. Facebook and Twitter light up with birth announcements, pictures and the cute things babies do. New babies bring a smile to the face of people everywhere. The same should be true when people are born into God's family. Great celebration should take place. When we understand these are people God loves and for whom Jesus died. These are the people for whom God created the church. This is what the first century church got really excited about and the Pharisees got really upset about. This is what makes heaven rejoice. (Luke 15:7) "I say to you that likewise there will be more joy in heaven over one sinner who repents than over ninety-nine just persons who need no repentance." What makes heaven rejoice? People coming to Christ. I believe we need to keep heaven rejoicing.

I am often asked, "Does Revitalization of the church lead to more people coming to Christ, or will more people coming to Christ lead to greater revitalization?" I believe both are true. A greater burden leads to greater intentional evangelism. Intentional evangelism leads to a renewed church. The bottom line of joy is realized as Christians take seriously the mission of the church.

Chapter 9

Bringing Renewal to the Local Church

2 Chronicles 29:6-11

*T*his is the second in a series of renewal and renovation messages to challenge each of us individually and all of us corporately as a local church.

6 For our fathers were unfaithful and did what is evil in the sight of the LORD our God. They abandoned Him, turned their faces away from the LORD's tabernacle, and turned their backs on Him. 7 They also closed the doors of the portico, extinguished the lamps, did not burn incense, and did not offer burnt offerings in the holy place of the God of Israel. 8 Therefore, the wrath of the LORD was on Judah and Jerusalem, and He made them an object of terror, horror, and mockery, as you see with your own eyes. 9 Our fathers fell by the sword, and our sons, our daughters, and our wives are in captivity because of this. 10 It is in my heart now to make a covenant with Yahweh, the God of Israel so that His burning anger may turn away from us. 11 My sons, don't be negligent now, for the LORD has chosen you to stand in

> *His presence, to serve Him, and to be His ministers*
> *and burners of incense."* [52]

In a previous message we looked at the earlier verses of this chapter in 2 Chronicles and at the actions of young Hezekiah who ascended to the throne in Judah at the age of 25. In order to remind you this king inherited the throne from his father King Ahaz. Ahaz was a wicked king who had practiced, established and promoted idol worship. The Lord's anger was raised and the people were suffering because of the actions of the King and the idolatry of the nation. I believe that it is apparent that what Hezekiah did in Judah is what is needed in many churches today. If we are going to renovate the church we must: Repair what is fractured and remove what does not fit.

Often while churches rush around and race around trying to renovate the church today, it is easy to miss the things necessary to revitalize the church. There are some things within the church that are broken and need to be *repaired*. There are some things within the church that are missing that need to be *replaced*. There are some things within the church that simply do not belong in a church that need to be *removed*. There are some things within the church that have been *neglected*. There are some things within the church that need to be *recognized* as hurting the church's chances for growth and health. We need to look at the need for God's restoration of the church today. The Church in the Western Hemisphere and particularly in North America is in critical need of renovation and revitalization. The church of the past full of health and vigor is no longer that same church and it is a mere shell of itself. Churches today all across the west are in need of church revitalization and renewal. I want to speak to you today on the subject: *Brining Renewal to the Local Church*.

Hezekiah did not excuse himself or his generation when he described the sins of their fathers. Rather, he asserted that the nation must acknowledge its corporate guilt and take steps to rectify what had been done. Admitting that one's nation and cultural heritage have

---

[52] The Holy Bible: Holman Christian Standard Version. (Nashville: Holman Bible Publishers, 2009), 2 Chronicles 29:6–11.

turned away from God is not easy, but true repentance must place the glory of God above national and family pride.

I. Realize What Is Forgotten (vs.6-7)

Hezekiah said:

> *For our fathers have trespassed, and done that which was evil in the eyes of the LORD our God, and have forsaken him, and have turned away their faces from the habitation of the LORD, and turned their backs. 7 Also they have shut up the doors of the porch, and put out the lamps, and have not burned incense nor offered burnt offerings in the holy place unto the God of Israel.*

As he addresses the Priests & Levites, Hezekiah explained, "Their ancestors were unfaithful and did what was evil in the sight of the Lord:

"They turned their backs on the Lord"
"They abandoned His temple"
"They shut the doors to the Temple's entry room"
"They snuffed out the lamps"
"They stopped burning incense"
"And they ceased presenting burnt offerings at the sanctuary"

It is easy to come to a place within a church where we begin to neglect some of the most important things in church. We forget to keep evangelism as the single most important priority in the church. We forget that the church is not for those of us who come regularly, but for those not yet reached with the gospel. We forget that we must stay relevant to the younger generations if we are going to draw them to the church. We forget that in order for our children's children to want to come to our church, the things which we like the most about our church, are the very things which are repelling the young. We forget that while we are comfortable with being comfortable in our

121

church with the way we do things, these things may be the very reason we are plateaued or in rapid decline.

In verse 6 it says that our Fathers have trespassed, Ahaz, and his contemporaries have turned back, not looking towards rising sun,[53] as Ezekiel 8:16 says:

> So He brought me to the inner court of the LORD's house, and there were about 25 men at the entrance of the LORD's temple, between the portico and the altar, with their backs to the LORD's temple and their faces turned to the east. They were bowing to the east in worship of the sun.[54]

They forgot the dwelling of the Lord and they turned their backs on God. When Hezekiah became the King, he set to work righting what was forgotten. He made the necessary decisions required. He did not summon the priests & Levites and ask for them to develop a plan to make things better. Hezekiah did not do what so many churches do today and copy what someone else is doing. He just kept leading like he should lead. Guiding the people as he was called to do. Directing the people of God towards the things of God. He realized what his father had forgotten. He sought to draw the people back to God and to remind them of that which they had forgotten. What were the forgotten things the people allowed? They forgot:

- To keep themselves committed to the holiness of God (vs. 6a).
- To keep the Lord first and foremost in their lives (vs. 6b).
- To keep worshipping in the Lord's house weekly (vs. 6c).
- To keep the house of God looking beautiful and open.
- To continue to receive offerings for the work of the ministry.

---

[53] James Wolfendale, I & II Chronicles, The Preacher's Complete Homiletic Commentary (New York; London; Toronto: Funk & Wagnalls Company, 1892), 277–278.

[54] The Holy Bible: Holman Christian Standard Version. (Nashville: Holman Bible Publishers, 2009), Ezekiel 8:16.

We can be just like the people of God during Hezekiah's reign and forget the real things that matter. God has not left us nor forsaken us and we need to recommit ourselves to those things of God which have always worked.

In verse seven we read:

They also closed the doors of the portico, extinguished the lamps, did not burn incense, and did not offer burnt offerings in the holy place of the God of Israel.

King Ahaz eliminated the ritual responsibilities that were part of the worshipping community. He reversed the pattern of worship that Solomon initiated and on which his son Abijah continued.[55] Hezekiah's task was the restoration of these earlier patterns practiced by Solomon.

For so many churches the words restoration and revitalization means growing in numbers, noises, and nickels. Some churches want to become all things to all people as they compromise on the tenants of God. Some hope to please the masses by watering down the Gospel so everyone is not called to repentance. There are no man made techniques towards revival that will help revitalize the church. What does revitalization mean?

Every place I go people ask me for a definition of church revitalization. Church Revitalization is a movement within protestant evangelicalism, which emphasizes the missional work of turning a plateau or rapidly declining church around and moving it back towards growth. It is lead through a Church Revitalization Initiative, which is when a local church begins to work on the renewal of the church with a concerted effort to see the ministry revitalized and the church become healthy. Church Revitalization means that the local church knew how, at one time previously, to renew, revitalize, and re- establish the health and vitality of the ministry. One of the challenges for the laity in the day in which we live is that they have lost the knowledge of church renewal and no longer want to cultivate the skill sets necessary to see their church experience revitalization.

---

[55] C.f. 2 Chronicles 13:11.

Even sadder is when a congregation does not have the corporate memory that there was a day when the local church was reaching people for Christ Jesus and active as evangelistic witnesses into their community. We must realize what has been forgotten and return to these things.

I remember a church, which I pastored and was being revitalized and renewed. We had grown and were in need of refurbishing the sanctuary. During the months that progressed, as we worked towards remodeling and refurbishing the sanctuary, it amazed me who was angered by the process. We had to remove a certain number of pews each month in order for them to be restored and repainted and stained. It was not the active membership, which were enraged, but those who either no longer attended or had left the church for another one with less emphasis of the inerrancy of scripture. I would have thought that our church's need for a fresh look as we continued to grow would be received with great excitement. They were enraged because they had given monies towards these pews and in their belief that gave them the right to allow the pews to remain in disarray because a former family member sat in that pew. I was excited because we were reaching people in the community and our present membership was reunited and advancing forward with the message of Christ. Yet there were those outside of the church which were unhappy. While they had long since lost their right to speak into the issues, they nevertheless tried to trash our church for repairing the previously forgotten facilities.

Where I serve in central Florida and for that matter all over North America there are churches closing their doors because they will not make the necessary changes to keep the church from ceasing to exist. There are thousands of churches that close their doors each year. These are in terrible circumstances and if they do not allow us to help them, they will not survive much longer. These churches were once bright places full of God's anointing and blessings. Yet, now they struggle to keep the doors open. They have forgotten what needs to be repaired. Are there some things which might need to be repaired in your life today?

II. We Must Recognize the Fury of the Lord – vs. 8-9

Therefore, the wrath of the LORD was on Judah and Jerusalem, and He made them an object of terror, horror, and mockery, as you see with your own eyes. Our fathers fell by the sword, and our sons, our daughters, and our wives are in captivity because of this.

Hezekiah clarifies the significance of the situation as he addresses the Priests and Levites. He says that the wicked actions of the leaders and the people have ignited the fury of the Lord. There were some severe consequences as a result of their sin: The men had been killed in battle and the sons and daughters and wives have been captured. The current situation was desperate. The condition of Judah and Jerusalem was comparable to the situation in the north.[56] The anger of the Lord made Judah and Jerusalem *"an object of dread and horror and scorn,"* language used elsewhere of the exiles in Babylon.[57] J. A. Thompson in the New American Commentary says, "the Chronicler's audience would not have missed the comparison and the applicability of Hezekiah's call to purity and unity of worship."[58]

Because of the sins of the fathers they had experienced His wrath. Because the rest of the people followed in their ways they too were experiencing God's wrath. Hezekiah proclaimed that the Lord *"has made them an object of dread, horror, and ridicule."* You can blame our problems with the country on the political leaders. You can blame the problems with this church or any other church on the leaders. But when you refuse to take a stand for what is right, then you become guilty as well. And there are consequences that will come, and you may be experiencing those consequences right now! Today, more than ever we need the revitalization and renewal of our churches all across the land.

---

[56] C.f. 2 Chronicles 28:9, 11, 13.

[57] C.f. Jeremiah 29:18; Jeremiah 19:8; 25:9, 18; 34:17; and Ezekiel 23:46.

[58] J. A. Thompson, 1, 2 Chronicles, vol. 9, The New American Commentary (Nashville: Broadman & Holman Publishers, 1994), 344–346.

If we are going to bring renewal to the local church, we must recognize the fury of the Lord. It is because of the sins of the children of God that the world is no longer attracted to the gospel message as it had been before. It is because of the sins of the children of God that those who need to be discipled are not being discipled in the local church. It is because of the sins of the children of God that the lost are not coming to saving knowledge of Jesus Christ. It is because of the sins of the children of God that the Holy Spirit is grieved and the Son is blasphemed. It is because of the sins of the children of God that our Heavenly Father is dishonored. It is because of the sins of the children of God that the fury of the Lord is ignited.

When will we wake up and take the actions necessary to turn from our sins and do what is right in the eyes of the Lord. We must: **realize what is forgotten, recognize the fury of the Lord, and we must restore what has fizzled out.**

III. We Must Restore What Has Fizzled Out – vs. 10–11.

> *It is in my heart now to make a covenant with Yahweh, the God of Israel so that His burning anger may turn away from us. My sons, don't be negligent now, for the LORD has chosen you to stand in His presence, to serve Him, and to be His ministers and burners of incense."*

Here Hezekiah begins a new element in his exhortation with the repeated introductory particle "now."[59] Hezekiah, as the leader of the nation, would stand in their behalf to seek to turn back the wrath of God against Israel. In this he was like Moses, interceding for the people.[60] Hezekiah expressed his intention of taking a solemn oath to put right what was wrong. It was not a renewal of the covenant between God and Israel, but a commitment by the king and the nation to seek

---

[59] C.f. Hebrew Word "attâ.

[60] C.f. Numbers 14:11–19.

God again with all their heart. Remarkably, Hezekiah's first response to the Assyrian threat was to return to the proper worship of God. Wilcock's comment is perceptive and applicable:

> When there is a financial crisis, the first thing we think about is money. When there is a communications crisis, our prime concern is to learn how to talk the language of the modern generation. When there is a church attendance crisis, we make it our chief aim to get numbers up. If Hezekiah had responded to a military threat in a military way, the Assyrians would have understood that. Army would have been matched against army, with dire consequences for Judah. But instead he and his people first looked up to God.

To be sure, Hezekiah also made practical military preparations for the coming siege.[61] We might say that he prayed hard and then he worked hard. But he put his prayers in the first place.

Notice that the clergy here in verse eleven had long neglected their duty and needed encouragement. The time had come for renewal. The fact that the ministry of the temple had fallen on bad times did not mean that it had to stay that way. Again the verse is introduced in Hebrew by the important term "now, "since this is his concluding exhortation. The command he gave them at the beginning in verse five must be followed with all diligence and haste because the Lord had entrusted to them the responsibility of temple worship. Hezekiah has taken the proper steps to repair those things that had been broken. He ensured that everything that didn't belong in the Temple and in the Kingdom was removed. He encountered the Priests and Levites and addressed the consequences that were happening as a result of the idolatry. The young king now tackles what we must restore what has fizzled out.

Some of the things which have fizzled out might be ones relationship with God. Hezekiah was going to claim God's promise that was recorded in 2 Chronicles 7:14-16:

---

[61] C.f. 2 Chronicles 32:1–5.

¹⁴ If My people who are called by My name humble themselves, pray and seek My face, and turn from their evil ways, then I will hear from heaven, forgive their sin, and heal their land.¹⁵ My eyes will now be open and My ears attentive to prayer from this place.¹⁶ And I have now chosen and consecrated this temple so that My name may be there forever; My eyes and My heart will be there at all times.⁶²

When it comes to **restoring what has fizzled out**, we must start with our relationship with the Holy God. Here is a church revitalization lesson each and every single one of us must get. Here it is: We will never see revitalization within the Church, until the people of God restore the things which have fizzled out in our spiritual walks so we can get back to being right with the Lord. This is what Hezekiah prescribed to the Priests and Levites. He told them to *"purify themselves"* first. God is in the restoration business and He will honor the promise of 2 Chronicles 7:14 if we will turn from our sins to him, ten will he hear, forgive, and heal.

Some of the things which have fizzled out might be ones relationship with God.

It might also involve one renewed commitment to serve the Lord. Hekekiah says in verse eleven:

"My sons, don't be negligent now, for the LORD has chosen you to stand in His presence, to serve Him, and to be His ministers and burners of incense."

Hezekiah says to them do not be negligent for the Lord has chosen you. He reminds them that they were chosen for this specific task—*"the LORD has chosen you to stand in His presence, to serve Him, and to be His ministers."* Have you allowed other things and life's circumstances to keep you from serving the Lord? You are not letting the minister down. You are not letting the church leadership

---

⁶² *The Holy Bible: Holman Christian Standard Version.* (Nashville: Holman Bible Publishers, 2009), 2 Ch 7:14–16.

down. You have let the Lord down because you have failed to offer service to him. It is the Lord who has called you and chosen you to serve him. It is time to restore what has fizzled out.

When we as individuals restore what has fizzled out, then we can begin the process of bringing renewal to the local church. These men obeyed their King. Then they reached out and carried that message to others. They gathered their brethren, and sanctified themselves, and came, according to the commandment of the king, by the words of the Lord, to cleanse the house of the Lord. Rather than a few people assuming the load, now there were many together ready to do what was commanded. What is most significant is the fact that all of these people got together and did things God's way. This church and most churches in the western hemisphere need revitalization and renewal.

Samuel Medley wrote a wonderful poem entitled the Living Stone: On Christ salvation rest secure:

The Rock of Ages must endure;
Nor can that faith be overthrown
Which rests upon the Living Stone.
No other hope shall intervene;
To Him we look, on Him we lean;
Other foundations we disown
And build on Christ, the Living Stone.
In Him it is ordained to raise
A temple to Jehovah's praise;
Composed of all the saints who own
No Savior but the Living Stone.
View the vast building, see it rise;
The work how great! the plan how wise!
Oh, wondrous fabric! power unknown!
That raises its work on the Living Stone.

We must Realize What Is Forgotten, We Must Recognize the Fury of the Lord, and We Must Restore What Has Fizzled Out.

Chapter 10

Be the Church in Practice

Joshua 3:1-8

A s followers of Christ, how do we turn 'church' into more than just a one hour a week event? How can we turn 'church' into a lifestyle? Church is not something we attend; it's something we are.

As followers of Christ, we are the church. When we leave the church building we don't leave church and pick it up again next week. Wherever we go we are the church. The church is defined as the body of Jesus Christ. Who is the head of the church? It's Christ, and we are the body. Therefore as the body of Christ we are representatives of Christ in the world. Where we live, work and play every day, we are to be the church, the body of Christ, in practice.

The word practice can be defined two ways. The word practice can mean *to prepare for something*. You may practice your piano lessons in preparation for a recital. Or you practice baseball preparing for a baseball game that you're going to play. That's one meaning of the word practice. Another meaning of the word practice is *to put into action*. For example, a doctor practices medicine. That doesn't mean the doctor practices on you in order to learn something. It means the doctor puts into action his or her God-given skills, education, and medical training to affect a positive change in your body. That's the meaning of the word practice that we will use as we look at being the church in practice.

When we talk about the church in practice, we're not preparing for something, but rather we are doing something. We are being something. We are the church in action. Our relationship with Christ is meant to be lived out in the world where we live every day. We're only at church an hour, or two or more a week, depending on what activity we're involved in. But we live many hours out in the world, on the job, in our neighborhoods, at home, and other places. As followers of Christ, our relationship with Him is meant to be lived out, put into action in these daily activities.

There are two dangers we face as Christians. One is to look at church as something we do for an hour or two each week, and think of that activity as church. We talk about 'going to church'. We must be careful not to reduce the idea of 'church', to the one or two hours a week that we're inside the church building. Another danger is allowing a subtle air of superiority to creep into our lives. This happens with a lot of growing Christians, especially when they get really excited about God. All of a sudden this subtle air of superiority appears and it's not attractive to others. We are to be salt and light, drawing people to Christ, not hot chili pepper repelling people from Him. That's not the kind of Christianity God wants us to live out in the world. We're not to reduce church to an activity and we're not to act superior. We must remember we are recipients of God's Grace. That's all we are. As recipients of God's Grace we are to live out the grace life before others so that people can see Jesus Christ in and through us. It requires faith to be the church in practice. Joshua 3:1-8 is a great illustration of the type of faith that's required of us if we are going to be the church in practice.

> *"Then Joshua rose early in the morning; and they*
> *set out from Acacia Grove and came to the Jordan,*
> *he and all the children of Israel, and lodged there*
> *before they crossed over. So it was, after three days,*
> *that the officers went through the camp; and they*
> *commanded the people, saying, "When you see the*
> *Ark of the Covenant of the* LORD *your God, and the*

> *priests, the Levites, bearing it, then you shall set*
> *out from your place and go after it. Yet there shall*
> *be a space between you and it, about two thousand*
> *cubits by measure. Do not come near it that you may*
> *know the way by which you must go, for you have*
> *not passed this way before." And Joshua said to the*
> *people, "Sanctify yourselves, for tomorrow the LORD*
> *will do wonders among you." Then Joshua spoke to*
> *the priests, saying, "Take up the Ark of the Covenant*
> *and cross over before the people." So they took up*
> *the Ark of the Covenant and went before the people.*
> *And the LORD said to Joshua, "This day I will begin*
> *to exalt you in the sight of all Israel, that they may*
> *know that, as I was with Moses, so I will be with you.*
> *You shall command the priests who bear the Ark of*
> *the Covenant, saying, 'When you have come to the*
> *edge of the water of the Jordan, you shall stand in the*
> *Jordan.'"* (Joshua 3:1-8, NKJV)[63]

The underlying theme in this passage is twofold. First, it requires faith to enter new territory with God and second, God gives us faith as we walk with Him. A great biblical example of what this looks like in a person's life is believer's baptism. One of the first steps to growth in Christ for a new believer is identifying with Him in baptism. Following Him, stepping into the baptismal water is new territory and it requires faith.

God gives us faith as we walk with him and our faith increases as we walk. Sometimes we have a tendency to pray something like this, "Oh God, give us more faith." And God responds, "Just start walking." He told the people to take up the Ark and start walking towards the Jordan River. That took faith. As they got closer to the swollen river it required even more faith to step into the water. As they walked with God in obedience, their faith increased.

---

[63] Scripture quotations are taken from the New King James Version (Nashville, TN: Thomas Nelson Inc., Publishers, 1979, 1980, 1982).

What kind of faith is required for us to be the church? It will require the faith to choose between the past and the future. In this passage Israel was poised on the edge of the property that God had promised them many years earlier. Only two of the original adults were alive to see this happen, Joshua and Caleb. Rewind to forty years earlier, Israel had been at this very point. God promised to give them this new territory. He wanted them to move in and take possession of the land. But the Israelites refused to enter the land at that time and as a result they were sent back into the wilderness where they lived for forty more years. They had to choose between the past, what was behind them and the future, what was before them.

The wilderness was the only way of life these people knew. They lived there for many years. It was a tough place, but it had also been a place for some good things. While in the wilderness God manifested Himself to them. They learned God was a powerful God. God's Word came to them as Moses went up the mountain and brought back the tablets, the Ten Commandments. They also experienced God's provision. God fed them and provided water for them. They had learned a lot about God while wandering in the wilderness. That's where they had lived their lives. But now God says move forward there's new territory.

It's so easy to become comfortable with the past that we refuse to move forward into new territory. It can happen in the life of an individual and it can happen in a church's life. It is easy to find security in the past. If we're not careful we will allow the past to keep us from experiencing what God has for us in the future.

God wanted the Israelites to move into this new territory. They had been at this river forty years earlier. God told them to go in and take possession of the land. He warned them that there would be enemies over there. God promised to drive them out, but He warned the Israelites that these enemies are not going to roll over and play dead. God told them they would have to go in and battle them in order to overcome them. Entering new territory always involves some battles. Whatever the new territory may be, it's going to require some battles. Every time we move forward there's going to be battles. Israel was not willing to battle for the new territory God promised them.

133

Instead they chose the comforts of the past. They were familiar with the wilderness and that's where they would live for forty more years.

For eighteen plus years our church did an event called *Starlight*. After eighteen years we decided to change the name to *Life Quest*. We also changed the location. We received a lot of positive feedback from many people. Nevertheless, we had to battle. We had to battle the "we've always called it *Starlight*." Somewhere in the book of Nehemiah it says, thou shall call it *Starlight*. Which, it doesn't. Moving forward we thanked God for the lives that were changed during the eighteen plus years of *Starlight*, but we were determined to look out the windshield and thank God for the lives that are going to be changed during the new event, *Life Quest*. Entering new territory always involves battles.

The second thing we've got to do when we're entering new territory is keep our eyes on Christ. If we're going to have the faith to move into the future, cross the rivers that God places in front of us, we've got to keep our eyes on Christ.

> *"And they commanded the people, saying, "When you see the Ark of the Covenant of the LORD your God, and the priests, the Levites, bearing it, then you shall set out from your place and go after it."*

The Ark of the Covenant is representative of God's presence and power. We do not have a physical Ark of the Covenant today to follow. Our Ark of the Covenant is the Lord Jesus Christ and we follow Him. In this passage we are reminded to keep our eyes on Him. Two things he says do: follow at a distance and don't get too close. Now that's surprising. We've always been taught to following as close to Christ as we can. Spiritually speaking, absolutely. If we're going to make it in this world, we need to tie tightly to Christ. But there's another aspect to this that we've got to understand.

> *"Yet there shall be a space between you and it, about two thousand cubits by measure. Do not come near it that you may know the way by which you must go, for you have not passed this way before."*

134

He spells it out. We've never been this way before. He's saying there are so many people and the Ark is in front of you. Don't crowd around so those in the back can't see the Ark. We've got to give some room. There's a New Testament story that correlates with this. It's a story about four men who care about their paralyzed friend very much, and they want to get him to Jesus. Jesus is teaching in a very crowded house. They go to the front door and there are all these people packed in this home to see Jesus and no one will let them in. They just keep crowding around the door blocking this man out. Rather than being discouraged and quitting, these men go up on the roof and cut a hole in the roof so they can lower their friend into the house. There was probably someone sitting in that room that looked up and said, "Hey, I can't believe they're cutting a hole in our roof. We've never done it that way before. It must be some young person up there cutting a hole in the roof." This verse is about not standing in the way of what God wants to do. We're either going to be in the way or we're going to be on the way. God is calling us to commit to be on the way. If that means cutting some holes in some roofs, we need to cut some holes in some roofs in order to see what God wants to do.

The second thing he's saying here is that we must not to lose sight of Him. Walking in faith leads us to walk in places we've never walked before. When we start walking places we've never been before, we need to keep our eyes on the Lord Jesus Christ. We are entering new territory; we must keep our eyes open and fixed on Jesus.

A few years ago our church started a new ministry called *Celebrate Recovery* [64]. It's a ministry that's a genuine instrument of compassion and the love of Jesus to people who are dealing with some type of hurt, habit or hang-up in their life. Starting a new ministry like this required tremendous boldness to walk where we've never been before. When we first started this ministry, there were those who were skeptical and wondered "What in the world are they doing now?" We kept our eyes on Jesus. We were willing to cut some holes in the roof and we were willing to walk into the river. After one year of starting this new ministry, we had a celebration. We celebrated

---

[64] CELEBRATE RECOVERY® **A Christ-Centered Recovery Program, www. celebraterecovery.com.**

many lives that were liberated in this ministry through the power of Jesus Christ. God blessed our commitment, as a church, to boldly follow Him into the new territory of not just going to church, but being the church. When we keep our eyes on Jesus and we're willing to be on the way, instead of in the way, God will do great things.

Number three, we must expect God to do great things. Look at verse five.

> *"Sanctify yourselves, tomorrow the Lord will do wonders among you."*

Rather than merely reflecting on what God has done we must also anticipate what He will do. In other words, don't lose the awe factor. He says, "The Lord will do wonders."

Number four, we must act in faith.

> *"Command the priests who bear the Ark of the Covenant saying when you come to edge of the water of the Jordan River, stand in it."*

God had parted waters on one other occasion, the Red Sea. Joshua and Caleb were the only adults still living that witnessed this incredible event. These people had never seen God part waters. God is saying to them go stand in that river. These people were not swimmers. They've been in the wilderness, the desert, for forty years. Here was this river and it was at a time of the year when the river was swollen and overflowing its banks. Visualize the water rushing before them, and God says, "Go stand in it." The difference between this experience and the Red Sea experience, God told Moses to stand on the shore line of the Red Sea, lift the rod of God to the heavens so He could part the waters and allow them to walk through on dry ground. This time God tells them to go stand in the river and then He will part the waters.

The Red Sea parting of the waters certainly is more appealing than the Jordan River deal. This stepping into the river stuff requires more faith. God will always do mighty things, but He doesn't always do them the same way. There was most likely that same person in that crowd that day shouting, "No, no, no! We're members of the church that has waters already parted before we cross rivers. That's the way it's always been done. God always parts the waters first. We've read about it." God tells them, "Go stand in the river." Don't wait on some sign, step into the river. When we do, God is going to do a new thing.

What does it take to step into the river? One, it takes courage to step into the river. It took courage for the priest to step into the river before God parted the water. Two, it takes a willingness on our part to fight the battles that will come. There's always going to be battles. Three, it's going to take a willingness to take on the challenger, even when others are not willing. It takes us, being willing, even when others are not.

Forty years earlier ten were unwilling to enter the land but two were willing. They took a vote. Ten voted no and two voted yes. They decided to go with the majority and it cost them a forty-year wilderness experience. The church needs leaders who are willing, ready and able to step into the river and see what God wants to do next. Church, are we ready to get into the river and see what God wants to do next? God is up to something great. It's time for us to see what He wants to do. Step into the river, trust Him, obey Him, and see what He will do next.

Chapter 11

Reclaiming the One That Goes Astray!

Matthew 18:12-14

> *12 What do you think? If a man has 100 sheep, and
> one of them goes astray, won't he leave the 99 on the
> hillside and go and search for the stray? 13 And if
> he finds it, I assure you: He rejoices over that sheep
> more than over the 99 that did not go astray. 14 In the
> same way, it is not the will of your Father in heaven
> that one of these little ones perish.*[65]

I would like for us to focus upon the heart of a Church
Revitalizer for revitalization and renewal for reclaiming
the one that goes astray. I believe it is time for protestant evangelical leaders across this land to commit to going after the one church
that goes astray. We have spent the last twenty years placing a huge
emphasis on the panting of churches only to discover that while the
new churches are surviving a little over 60 percent of the time, the
existing church is struggling to regain its health and vitality. If we
do not begin to add the revitalization and renewal of churches to the
equation, what we will be left with are fewer and fewer churches

---

[65] The Holy Bible: Holman Christian Standard Version. (Nashville: Holman Bible
Publishers, 2009), Matthew 18:12–14.

across the landscape of the western hemisphere and a population which is drifting even further from the things of God.

Although this passage was originally intended for individuals, there is a principle here, which should not be over looked. Here is the principle: If the Lord is interested in the one individual sheep that goes astray, it is indeed possible that He is also interested in the single church, which faces the same challenge. A case can be made that this passage has relevance as well for the local church. The heart of the great Shepherd leaves the ninety-nine to seek to reclaim the one who went astray. The underlying principle and the reason it is relevant to church revitalization, is that the one lost sheep outside the fold calls for a higher degree of concern than the ninety-nine inside. With the seeking of the one that has been led astray, we get to the heart of the parable as well as the church revitalizer. This certainly shows the priority Jesus placed on reaching outside to those who are lost, with those already in the fold.

David Dockery states that Jesus in Matthew 18:10-14 explained why He can command these things of His followers when he declares, "God has already demonstrated the ultimate humility in leaving His nearly complete flock of ninety-nine sheep to seek to recover one stray."[66] Luke in his Gospel version recorded in Luke15:6 gives a questioning form to the parable by beginning, *"Which man of you?"* The rhetorical question implies a positive response in the Greek: *of course that is the way one would act.* The point of the parable is the disproportionate investment of effort and concern directed towards the one sheep. The one is momentarily of more importance than the ninety-nine. The lost one of the flock and its restoration is vital to the shepherd above the ninety-nine safe and secure in the fold. Jesus is now not laying down a strong declaration of his own, but calling on those listening to him to work something out for themselves. He refers to a man who owns a flock of *"a hundred sheep"* of which *"one goes astray."* Such a man does not reason that 99 percent of his flock is safe and well and that on the whole he has no reason for alarm.

---

[66] Dockery, David S. Ray Van Neste, and Jerry Tidwell, Southern Baptist Evangelicals and the Future of Denominationalism. (Nashville: B&H Publishing Group, 2011), 558-59.

Vital to this passage is to show what the shepherd will do, when even one of His sheep is lost. He seeks to find it. Notice the reluctance of the shepherd to lose it. Revitalization and renewal is saying we must not let the church just drift away into obscurity. Let's look at the subject today of reclaiming the one that goes astray!

1. The Whole One Hundred Are Happy and Comfortable–vs. 1.

We begin with the depiction of an entire flock of sheep happy and comfortable doing things that sheep do day in and day out. To demonstrate the Father's concern for every believer, Jesus tells a parable in which the significance of even one sheep or one church for that matter that has gone astray, becomes the object of intense concern. If we are to look at the churches all across our country as the happy flock, there are many who are entirely comfortable with those who are presently part of it. For the ninety-nine, there is little emphasis on reaching out to those who have gone astray or those who are not yet children of God. Look at verse one with me:

> *12 What do you think? If a man has 100 sheep, and one of them goes astray, won't he leave the 99 on the hillside and go and search for the stray?*

Jesus uses a parable, setting up an imagined sheep-owner who has one hundred sheep in his flock. It sounds quite strange to consider that a shepherded would leave ninety-nine who are all connected and leave the majority of the flock to track down one lost sheep. Notice that the ninety-nine are in no danger. They are clearly safe, secure, and obedient believers. But one is in danger and the one is a sheep who has left the safety of the flock and the shepherds care and is at great risk and vulnerable.

2. The Ninety-Nine are Fine, But One is in Danger – vs. 1b.

Now the ninety and nine are left. The ninety-nine refer to faithful followers of Jesus who no longer need to repent because they are not straying from him. Absolutely Christ does not leave his true sheep. But special care is needed to find the one, which is lost. In our churches today there are those who are perfectly content with just doing the same old thing in the same old way expecting the same old results. When one falls away they just shrug their shoulders and say, "they really were not one of us." Churches, which are dealing with the need to be revitalized, display a mutual selfishness in participants who would enjoy the luxuries of devotion in such a way as to hinder the work of saving the lost of those who feel pushed out. Declining churches are filled with comfortable worshippers, unresponsive parishioners, declining congregants who in some situations hold the place they sit each Sunday more as private possessions than public arenas for the lost to gather. When that is the norm the stranger, the visitor, and the neighbor feel they are not welcomed and will drift away.

Notice here in the passage that the one wandering sheep is a believer. Earlier in this Chapter they are referred to as: "*one of these little ones*" who wanders away from intimate fellowship of the church. In the Greek translation of the phrase "one of them," the same wording is employed as verses 5-6 and verse 10. It also appears in verse 14 as well. So it is clear that Jesus still has Christians rather than literal young people in mind. Leaving the ninety-nine does not suggest they are unguarded; other shepherds would have kept watch over them. At the spiritual level, of course, God is able to search for the wanderer even while still protecting those who have not strayed.

3. Reclaiming the One That Goes Astray – vs. 13

Look at verse 13:

> *13 And if he finds it, I assure you: He rejoices over that*
> *sheep more than over the 99 that did not go astray.*

The imagery of a good shepherd who pastorally cares for all the sheep recalls the language of Ezekiel 34"11-16 where it reads:

> "*the Sovereign LORD says: 'I myself will search for*
> *my sheep and look after them ...' ".*

141

Notice in this passage the fourfold sequence of the shepherd. *We see his departure to search for the lost sheep, His journey to reclaim the wondering sheep, The Shepherds success in finding the lost sheep, and the natural elation of saving that, which was lost.*

We see his departure to search for the lost sheep

The quest to reclaim the sheep is not sure to be rewarded. Just like it is not every wandering sinner, which is reclaimed by Christ, the same is true of the local declining church. Not every church even when it is in decline is committed to the revitalization and transformation of its congregation. Man's obstinacy makes the result of revitalization uncertain. Do you realize that there is a limit to the patience of the Lord? When we think of the individual, if a person will not open their heart to God and co-operate with the grace, which will prevent such a fall, then they will not be found and returned home. God forces no individual to be saved and no local declining church to be revitalized against their will.

His journey to reclaim the wondering sheep

The Shepherd's journey required him to travel far into a wasteful and difficult country. Sin leads its votaries into hungry solitudes and among fearful dangers. Christ follows the wandering soul. His journey into this world was his following, and his hard life and death his journeying over wild mountains. He follows each one now. He will not leave the lost to their fate. Even the local church which appears to be ready to surrender its fate to church closure can be turned around if the membership is ready to embrace new things or allow a group which works to restore churches through a restart to work with them.[67]

The Shepherds success in finding the lost sheep

The lost sheep is discovered. The shepherd made a sacrifice personally to go after the one, which went astray. The energy expounded to bring restoration was high. Preservation of the individual sheep or the individual church took real effort. The Lord Jesus desires to

---

[67] For more information regarding restarting a church or relaunching one go to **www.RenovateConference.org/resources** and look for the materials which will assist you in the decisions necessary to assure a new future.

bring back believers and bring back churches which have wandered away from Him.

The natural elation of saving that, which was lost

There is joy and natural elation at the restoration of one who has strayed away. This alone points to the significance of each sheep in the eyes of the shepherd. If the gospel is for any one, it is for the lost sheep. There is only one, yet it is a great trouble that even one should go astray. This displays the worth of an individual soul. This reveals the horrific evil of sin. The exhibits the lapse of but one man into so fearful a fall that it is enough to disarrange the whole order of the community.

It is in the finding and rescuing of one sheep gone astray that produces a greater joy than remaining with the ninety-nine who stayed in the security of the fold. For that reason the shepherd does not hesitate to focus his concern upon the lost sheep, in order to experience the joy of restoration. The Lord Jesus drew special attention to the Father's rejoicing with the phrase, I tell you the truth. He further heightened the Father's joy by associating it with His joy at the continual faithfulness of those who follow the path of righteousness. But understand, the Lord's delight with the ninety-nine faithful ones was not meant to be minimized in this passage. It was assumed that he was already greatly pleased with them, but he loved to display his saving grace toward those who were most undeserving. When God turns around a declining church which was once on the death throws of elimination, I believe there is that exact same joy that was felt in the return of a sheep to the fold.

Conclusion

The joy of Jesus Christ is the joy of saving the lost. No one may safely go on sinning, or living in careless unconcern, with the expectation of being finally found and saved. God takes the initiative to go to great lengths to bring back to Himself those who are estranged from Him. Reclaiming such people should lead to joyous celebration. The faithfulness of the majority may never excuse us for ignoring anyone who still remains distant from God. Practical applications require a strong emphasis on pastoral care within our churches; workable implementation strategies carefully structured and supervised networks of under shepherd lay leaders leading small groups, and other forms ministries.

The Body of Christ is accountable to the Shepherd to give unreserved commitment to restoring those who have fallen. The focus here is in restoring. Though only one has disappeared, the shepherd's whole routine is changed. He focuses all his energy on reclaiming the one that is lost. Vital to this passage is to show what the shepherd will do, when even one of His sheep is lost. He seeks to find it. Notice the reluctance of the shepherd to lose it. Church revitalization and renewal is saying we must not let the church just drift away into obscurity.

Can you think my friends of someone who is drifting away from this church today? If so are you looking for them and calling them trying to minister to them? Do you want to see this church turned around and brought back to full vitality? What were the answers which just flashed through your mind?

Were you saying, Lord I will be part of the effort to turn around this church? Or were you one who said I just simply do not want to see this church brought back to life?

The first points towards possibilities, while the second points towards more problems of decline. The later aligns with the evil one and wants to do nothing to turnaround this church. The former is greeted by a loving Lord who is pursuing us today because he loves us. Run to the arms of the Lord and watch him turn around this church.

We see:

1. **The Whole One Hundred Are Happy and Comfortable**
2. **The Ninety-Nine are Fine, But One is in Danger**
3. **Reclaiming the One That Goes Astray**

I want us to be found in the reclamation business. Reclaiming lost souls. Reclaiming drifting souls. Reclaiming lost churches, which need to become healthy churches. Will you join me in the effort?

Chapter 12

The Power of Grace

Luke 15:11-32

The Parable of the Lost Sheep

"𝒯hen all the tax collectors and the sinners drew near to Him to hear Him. And the Pharisees and scribes complained, saying, "This Man receives sinners and eats with them." So He spoke this parable to them, saying: "What man of you, having a hundred sheep, if he loses one of them, does not leave the ninety-nine in the wilderness, and go after the one which is lost until he finds it? And when he has found it, he lays it on his shoulders, rejoicing. And when he comes home, he calls together his friends and neighbors, saying to them, 'Rejoice with me, for I have found my sheep which was lost!' I say to you that likewise there will be more joy in heaven over one sinner who repents than over ninety-nine just persons who need no repentance.

The Parable of the Lost Coin

"Or what woman, having ten silver coins, if she loses one coin, does not light a lamp, sweep the house, and search carefully until she finds it? And when she has found it, she calls her friends and neighbors together, saying, 'Rejoice with me, for I have found the piece which I lost!' Likewise, I say to you, there is joy in the presence of the angels of God over one sinner who repents."

The Parable of the Lost Son

Then He said: "A certain man had two sons. And the younger of them said to his father, 'Father, give me the portion of goods that falls to me.' So he divided to them his livelihood. And not many days after, the younger son gathered all together, journeyed to a far country, and there wasted his possessions with prodigal living. But when he had spent all, there arose a severe famine in that land, and he began to be in want. Then he went and joined himself to a citizen of that country, and he sent him into his fields to feed swine. And he would gladly have filled his stomach with the pods that the swine ate, and no one gave him anything. "But when he came to himself, he said, 'How many of my father's hired servants have bread enough and to spare, and I perish with hunger! I will arise and go to my father, and will say to him, "Father, I have sinned against heaven and before you, and I am no longer worthy to be called your son. Make me like one of your hired servants."' "And he arose and came to his father. But when he was still a great way off, his father saw him and had compassion, and ran and fell on his neck and kissed him. And the son said to him, 'Father, I have sinned against heaven and in your sight, and am no longer worthy to be called your son.' "But the father said to his servants, 'Bring out the best robe and put it on him, and put a ring on his hand and sandals on his feet. And bring the fatted calf here and kill it, and let us eat and be merry; for this my son was dead and is alive again; he was lost and is found.' And they began to be merry. "Now his older son was in the field. And as he came and drew near to the house, he heard music and dancing. So he called one of the servants and asked what these things meant. And he said to him, 'Your brother has come, and because he has received him safe and sound, your father has killed the fatted calf.' "But he was angry and would not go in. Therefore his father came out and pleaded with him. So he answered and said to his father, 'Lo, these many years I have been serving you; I never transgressed your commandment at any time; and yet you never gave me a young goat that I might make merry with my friends. But as soon as this son of yours came, who has devoured your livelihood with harlots, you killed the fatted calf for him.' "And he said to him, 'Son, you are always with me, and all that I have is yours. It was right that we should make merry and be glad, for your brother was dead and is alive again, and was lost and is found'" (Luke 15:11-32 NKJV).[68]

Grace is a wonderful word. Don't you love the sound of that word? People love the word so much they even use it in proper names. We have a new grand baby. We have three grandchildren, the twins, Ryleigh and Avery who are five and now their baby sister. Our daughter named her Aligrace. The day Aligrace was born I was given one job to do. My job was to take my camera and capture the twin's first encounter with their new born sister. So with my camera ready, the twins enter the room. Ryleigh, the twin girl, walks over to Aligrace, puts her arms around her very gently, kisses her gently on the forehead and whispers, "Aligrace, welcome to the family. Mommy says your name means a *gift from God*." Imagine the scene, grandmother is crying, mom is crying, the nurses are oooing and awing; it's just a very sweet, tender moment and we will cherish forever. Then Avery, the twin boy, walks over to Aligrace, gently puts his hands on Aligrace, looks her right in the eye and says, "Aligrace, I want a brother!" In a matter of thirty seconds, we went from earth to heaven and right back down again.

The word grace does mean a *gift from God*. I am so thankful that our God is a God of Grace. In Luke Chapter 15 we have one of the most beautiful pictures of Grace one will find anywhere. The chapter begins with the Pharisees, the religious elite, criticizing Jesus. They are criticizing Jesus for the type of people He is choosing to hang out with. In response to their critical remarks and harsh tones, Jesus looks at them and proceeds to tell them a series of stories. In fact, He tells three stories during this encounter and all three stories relate to lost things.

The first story is about a lost sheep. In Middle Eastern economy, sheep were considered a very valuable commodity, especially to the

---

[68] Scripture quotations are taken from the New King James Version (Nashville, TN: Thomas Nelson Inc., Publishers, 1979, 1980, 1982).

shepherd who has lost one. Jesus explains the situation saying if a man loses one sheep out of a hundred, he will go and pursue that one lost sheep until he finds it.

In the second story, Jesus tells us about a lady who loses a valuable coin. Historians explain that this coin is very valuable because it belonged in a garland of ten coins that a married woman would wear. A valuable piece of this garland was missing. It would be like a lady losing a diamond out of her wedding ring set. This lost coin is of great value to her. She is frantically looking for this lost coin and will not give up until she finds it.

Finally, Jesus describes a situation involving a lost boy and his journeys to and from a far country. Charles Dickens said, "This story is the greatest short story of all times." [69] I agree with Mr. Dickens' statement. This final story in this chapter is all about the power of grace. In this particular story a person is lost and we see the power of grace through three individuals, the younger son, the father, and the elder brother.

As we read this story we realize, **we all need grace**. In the beginning of the story the younger son says to his father "I want the inheritance that is coming to me." According to Jewish custom, that would have only been one-third of the father's inheritance. Also, an inheritance is typically given after the parent dies. In this case, the younger son cannot wait until his father passes. He wants his portion of the inheritance now.

This reminds me of something that happened at my house not too long ago. Our three children and son-in-law were at the house one evening and I noticed they were whispering among themselves. Being the nosey dad that I am, I thought to myself, I need to find out what this conversation is all about. It turns out they were discussing what each one wanted when my wife and I cease to exist on this earth. They were having a great discussion. As they were getting all excited about this, I thought to myself, am I dying and don't even know it? Finally I said, "Uh, guys, I'm here, in the room, what are you talking about?" They answered, "Well dad, we don't want to have to deal with all this when

---

[69] Graham Storey, *The Letters of Charles Dickens*, 12 vols. (Oxford: Clarendon Press, 2002).

you're gone, so we're just deciding now." My oldest daughter says, "I want this painting." The other daughter says, "I want this." My son and son-in-law are debating over who's going to get the fishing boat. Later that evening my wife and I were talking and we decided that we really did need to talk about this. "What are we going to do with their inheritance?" Immediately the answer came to us. We decided we are going to spend their inheritance, every single dime of it. We're going to leave them bills, nothing else. We'll teach them.

Similarly the young man in this story wanted his inheritance but he was not willing to wait until his father passed. Once he received his inheritance, he was out of there. But the truth of the matter is, long before he received his portion of the inheritance he had already departed spiritually and emotionally. His mind and heart departed long before he received his inheritance. And guess what? We are no exception. Long before we commit the act of sin, we depart in our thought life. Our thoughts move us in the direction of sin and our actions eventually follow.

This young man immigrates to the far country, away from family, faith, customs, traditions, all the things he once treasured. While in the far country, life begins to crash in on him and he finally comes to himself. He realizes he needs help. Can we relate to his story today in the twenty-first century? Absolutely. We all have some prodigal in us.

Bible scholars have discussed and debated this story for years. Some argue that the story is about people who do not know Christ and they are in the 'far country' of lostness. We need to seek that person out, share the gospel of Christ and bring them to Christ. Others contend that the story is not about a person who is lost, but rather a person who is a believer who has departed from the care and fellowship of the father. I tend to think that when Jesus told parables, He told parables that would connect with anyone. In this case, both points of view can be true.

No matter what you have done, no matter how far you have immigrated to the far country, God loves you. Our God is a God of Grace. Maybe, you are a believer and you've ended up in the far country. Maybe there was a time when you were under the umbrella of fellowship with the Father and it was a time when your relationship was good, healthy and strong. You remember a time of sweet fellowship. You could pick up the bible and the words would come alive. You would pray and know you were connecting with the Father and He was hearing and answering your prayers. But something happened. Maybe it was an experience in life. Maybe over a period of time there were things that were attractive to you in the world and you moved out from the umbrella of God's care. You're too embarrassed and you think there's no way God will ever forgive you. That's exactly where this young man was. He thought there was no way he could ever become what he was before he left home. He thought he could never again have the same relationship with the father he once had. The young man decides to return home, but only as a servant. He thinks after all he's done and where's he been, there's no way his father will ever accept him as a son again. He's not even going to ask.

If you're like me, after reading this story I have two questions. First, why would anyone leave a loving environment like the father in the first place? What was he thinking? I think the answer is that the voice of love is a very quiet voice. The voice of God's love doesn't scream at you. It's a very quiet, still, small voice, and it's competing with much louder, worldly voices that attract, woo, pull and draw you away to the far country. These loud voices plead with you to go out and prove something, prove you matter. Can I tell you something? Ignore those loud voices. Tune into the still, small voice of God that tells you don't have to prove you matter. You already matter.

The second question is, why is the far country not defined? The answer is quite simple. The far country can be anywhere. It can be the far country of lostness. It can also be the far country of the believer who has stepped outside the umbrella of God's authority and care and has made really bad choices. The young son has made some bad choices and is struggling with the understanding of God's Grace. Not only does he fail to grasp the fact that we all need grace, but he also struggles to comprehend that we have a father ready to show grace.

We have a father who is ready to show grace. Maybe you're wondering, when does the father first demonstrate Grace to the son? The father first demonstrates grace when he allows the son to leave home in the first place. According to Jewish law the father has the authority to demand the son not leave. But the father chose not to. What a beautiful demonstration of God's grace. He loves you enough that if you want to go into the far country though He pleads with you, He shows you that it's wrong, He will allow you to go if you choose. That's grace. Grace would not be grace if God didn't allow us to make those choices. The father's first demonstration of grace is when he allows his son to go.

The father's second demonstration of grace is seen when the son comes home. Grace does not give up. As long as the son was alive, grace awaited him. Grace is greater than our failures. Before we move on, let's look at something else in the story, the image of the father. The son coming home is a moving image, but even more moving is the image of the father running to the son. When you read the story, it says when the father saw the son at a great distance, he ran to him. The father ran towards the son and embraced him. The son carried the stains of the pig pen on him. The muck and mire of the pig pen were all over him. The father didn't run to him and say, "Keep your distance, I cannot touch you because you've touched swine." The scripture says the father ran to him. The father paid no attention to the muck, mire and swine. He had no thought of what the son had done. He embraced the son, wrapped his arms around him and said, "Son, I love you and I'm going to throw a party like you've never seen before, because my son who was lost is now found." That is what Grace is all about. If you take the first step to God in faith, He will run to you. He will embrace you.

I was talking to a young man in my office one day. He came to see me and he was so distraught. I had preached the previous Sunday on salvation and how God wants people to come to Christ and experience abundant life here on earth and eternal life in heaven. This young man said to me "Pastor Larry, I just don't think that's true for me." I said, "What is it in your life that keeps you from accepting God's grace?" I said, "There's something." He began crying and said, "Larry, there is something that has such a grip on me. When I go to bed at night I am so guilt ridden. When I go to sleep, guilt stands in the corner and in the middle of the night I awaken and it pounces right back on me again. And I feel so guilty." I said, "Look, I don't need to know, God knows, but I will tell you, God will forgive your sin." He said, "No, I need to tell you. There was a time in my life when something happened and I went through a bad experience and I cursed God. And I really talked negatively about God and I was so mean. There's no way God can forgive me for what I said. And there's no way God could ever forgive me for what I thought and God could never forgive me for how mean I acted towards Him." I just smiled at him. And I said, "Let me tell you this, it doesn't matter what you've done, it doesn't matter what you've said. God's grace has not given up on you. In fact, not only does He want you to come home today, He's out looking for you. And He's waiting on you to come home. If you want to, right now, in this office want to, you can experience the grace of God." Right there and then, that young man bowed his head and he said, "God, I am so sorry. I am so sorry." Just like the young man in the story. He said, "I've sinned against you. I'm not worthy. But God if you will just accept me, just love me, and if you will just forgive me." At that point, the forgiveness of God washed over him and when he said amen, I said a prayer with him. Instantaneously his countenance changed. He told me later that when he walked outside the sky had never looked so blue and the trees never looked so green. He said he never felt freer in his life. It was as if God had just reached down and took a weight off him.

There's a third part to the story that we cannot neglect. It's the story of the older son. **Grace imparted is not always Grace received**. Let's examine the older brother in verses 25-32. "Now his older son was in the field. And as he came and drew near to the house, he heard music and dancing. So he called one of the servants and asked what these things meant. And he said to him, 'Your brother has come, and because he has received him safe and sound, your father has killed the fatted calf.' "But he was angry and would not go in. Therefore his father came out and pleaded with him. So he answered and said to his father, 'Lo, these many years I have been serving you; I never transgressed your commandment at any time; and yet you never gave me a young goat that I might make merry with my friends. But as soon as this son of yours came, who has devoured your livelihood with harlots, you killed the fatted calf for him.' "And he said to him, 'Son, you are always with me, and all that I have is yours. It was right that we should make merry and be glad, for your brother was dead and is alive again, and was lost and is found.'"

The older brother could not understand his father's grace. His reaction is the definition of religion. I'm so glad Christianity is not a religion? A religion is man's attempt to reach God. Christianity is God reaching down to man. Christianity is God's Grace in action. It's God seeking out the lost. It is God seeking out the believer who has stepped out from under the umbrella of fellowship, even though they still have a relationship. The older brother could not understand this. I like what [70]David Jeremiah says about the older brother. He says, "There are two possibilities when you look at the older brother. One, he was a son but he was living like a servant. He thought he constantly had to prove himself and he could never experience grace. Or he was a sinner who thought he was a saint. Perhaps he thought, because he was physically at home that made him spiritually at home. That can be the picture of someone who sits in a church pew every Sunday. Physically, they are in a place of worship. They sing the songs, listen to the sermons and even pray. But spiritually they are far from God. Pride is as much the far country as is immorality. The older brother was filled with pride.

What can we take away from this message?

1. God's desire is to bring home anyone who is in the far country.
2. When grace is experienced, celebration should follow. I love sports, I'm a sports fanatic. When I go to a sporting event and my team scores or wins, I applaud. How much more should I applaud when someone comes to Christ?
3. We can never allow those who are already at home to cause us to ignore those who are in the far country. We can never adopt the philosophy that the church is about us. The church is about those in the far country whom we need to seek and bring home.

That is the Power of Grace.

---

[70] Dr. David Jeremiah, *Captured by Grace: No one is Beyond the Reach of a Loving God* (Nashville, TN: Thomas Nelson, Inc., 2006).

Chapter 13

When God Says Go,
But the Church Says No!

Genesis 35:1-15

*T*here is a story which is told of Oliver Cromwell, the soldier and statesman who led the parliamentary forces in the English Civil War of 1653. When this leader was sitting for his portrait to be painted, he commanded the artist with the following statement:

"Paint me just like I am, with my warts and all!"

What Cromwell was meaning was that we ought to be open and honest as we see ourselves and as we see others just like we are and they are.

I want us to look at an individual in the Old Testament that was that kind of person. He was not a perfect person to be sure. Yet, we see that The Lord God took this person just as he was, warts and all, and used him for His glory.

When it comes to the revitalization of a church today it is good to know that the Lord will use us for His glory and that should give us encouragement. He was not a super man and he did not live at a level of perfection that the rest of us cannot attain. This story is a story of belated obedience. Often as a church we are faced with this challenge. God says go and the church says no! So let's look at today what happens *When the Church Says No, But God Says Go*. Read with me Genesis 35:1-15 as we discover who this individual is.

35 God said to Jacob, "Get up! Go to Bethel and settle there. Build an altar there to the God who appeared to you when you fled from your brother Esau." 2 So Jacob said to his family and all who were with him, "Get rid of the foreign gods that are among you. Purify yourselves and change your clothes. 3 We must get up and go to Bethel. I will build an altar there to the God who answered me in my day of distress. He has been with me everywhere I have gone." 4 Then they gave Jacob all their foreign gods and their earrings, and Jacob hid them under the oak near Shechem. 5 When they set out, a terror from God came over the cities around them, and they did not pursue Jacob's sons. 6 So Jacob and all who were with him came to Luz (that is, Bethel) in the land of Canaan. 7 Jacob built an altar there and called the place God of Bethel because it was there that God had revealed Himself to him when he was fleeing from his brother. 8 Deborah, the one who had nursed and raised Rebekah, died and was buried under the oak south of Bethel. So Jacob named it Oak of Weeping. 9 God appeared to Jacob again after he returned from Paddan-aram, and He blessed him. 10 God said to him:

Your name is Jacob; you will no longer be named Jacob, but your name will be Israel. So He named him Israel. 11 God also said to him: I am God Almighty. Be fruitful and multiply. A nation, indeed an assembly of nations, will come from you, and kings will descend from you. 12 I will give to you the land that I gave to Abraham and Isaac. And I will give the land to your future descendants. 13 Then

God withdrew from him at the place where He had spoken to him. 14 Jacob set up a marker at the place where He had spoken to him—a stone marker. He poured a drink offering on it and anointed it with oil. 15 Jacob named the place where God had spoken with him Bethel.[71]

There are many times as a Church Revitalizer where you are asked to lead a church off of the plateau or rapid decline it is experiencing. Sometimes the people of the church will be open and ready to follow while there are other times where the rank and file for the remaining membership simply do not want to change and are only looking for a "Church Chaplain" to hold there hands and to turn the lights off when the last one is gone. Often there are times when the church says no, but God says go and it does not always mean that the people are unwilling. Sometimes it is the pastor who is unwilling.

As we look at the life of Jacob we can see one who just might be unwilling to initially go. The occurrence of the journey we have read from scripture is wrapped around Jacob's sons. The crime of his sons had made it essential that Jacob should leave Shechem and its neighborhoods. I actually doubt that if God had not shown up with the invitation to go back to Bethel, he would have gone. His entire life was an example of delayed obedience and encircled with sin. The good news of the Gospel is that we do not have to stay the way we are. No matter how many times we have failed the Lord, we can go home again if we truly repent and obey. It happened to Abraham,[72] Isaac,[73] David,[74] Jonah,[75] and Peter;[76] and now it is happening to Jacob.

---

[71] The Holy Bible: Holman Christian Standard Version. (Nashville: Holman Bible Publishers, 2009), Genesis 35:1–15.

[72] C.f. Genesis 13:1–4.

[73] C.f. Genesis 26:17.

[74] C.f. 2 Samuel 12.

[75] C.f. Jonah 3:1–3.

[76] C.f. John 21:15–19.

For several years, Jacob had lingered thirty miles away from Bethel and had paid dearly for his disobedience.[77] But now the Lord spoke to him and told him to move to Bethel and settle down there. Jacob already knew that Bethel was God's appointed place for him and his family (31:13), but he had been slow to obey. "Remember therefore from where you have fallen; repent and do the first works" (Rev. 2:5, NKJV).

Bethel was a word that had great meaning. Numerous events of Bible history occurred there. The name Bethel comes from the Hebrew *"beth,"* meaning house, and *"el,"* meaning God. Bethel means House of God. Bethel is the place where Jacob saw the angels of God ascending and descending on the ladder connecting heaven and earth. It was there that Jacob had his experience with God. It was there that Jacob came to know the Lord in a intimate way. It was there that Jacob was to be born again. It was there that Jacob became a new person. Let us look at what happens when God says go, but the church says no.

1. When God Says Go, But the Sinner Says No – vs.1 & 3.

Notice what the Lord said to Jacob in verses one and three:

> *God said to Jacob, "Get up! Go to Bethel and settle there. Build an altar there to the God who appeared to you when you fled from your brother Esau."*

> *"We must get up and go to Bethel. I will build an altar there to the God who answered me in my day of distress. He has been with me everywhere I have gone."*

Go to Bethel. Get going and moving forward towards that which I have called you. Settle there and make this your place of dwelling.

---

[77] If Jacob was seventy-seven years old when he left home, and since he remained twenty years with Laban, this means he was ninety-seven when he started for Bethel. Isaac was sixty years older than Jacob. Thus he was one hundred and fifty-seven when Jacob returned and still had twenty-three more years to live (35:28).

Build an altar there to the Lord. God has answered me in my days of suffering and it is God's will for my life and journey. God spoke here to Jacob. He had built an altar on the property he had bought near Shechem and had called it *"God the God of Israel."*[78] But God was not happy with this altar because He wanted him worshiping back at Bethel. The Lord reminded Jacob of his distracted situation over twenty years ago and how He had delivered him and blessed him. At Bethel, Jacob had made some vows to the Lord; and now it was time for him to fulfill them.

Many a Church Revitalizer gets distracted at times because the effort is hard and the days are long. The distraction pays a toll on them and some eventually feel it is easier to surrender to the church folk than it is to remain strong in the Lord and His direction. Much of the problems within the Christian life and within the local church results from the problem of partial obedience. John Maxwell taught me some twenty-five years ago, that partial obedience is disobedience. My youth minister son, Drew, often reminds me of that phrase I shared with him growing up. When we know what the Lord wants us to do, we better start doing it. Jacob had stopped doing what God had called for him to do. When we do not continue to obey God and complete His will for our lives, even all that we have done right in the past starts to die.

That which the Lord Jesus said to the church that met in the town of Sardis, He is saying to each one of us:

> *"Be watchful, and strengthen the things which remain, that are ready to die, for I have not found your works perfect [having been fulfilled] before God"* (Rev. 3:2, NKJV).

Jacob was the second of twins. Easu was the first born of the two twin brothers. I am sure as scripture points out that Jacob was always a little jealous of the older brother Easu which was to receive the inheritance and blessing of the father. Perhaps resentment became a large part of his reason he was so disobedient. In one premeditated

---

[78] C.f. Genesis 33:20.

committed act he stole the birthright from his brother. Easu is storming mad and threatens his younger brother because of what he had done.

So here is Jacob running from the father he had lied to, the brother he had stolen from, and the God who he had sinned against.

2. When God Says Go, But the Back Slider Says No – vs. 2.

Jacob had been a wealthy desert chieftain in Shechem. He was a wealthy nomad who had a five-pole tent signifying his importance. Even to this day the Bedouins still signify importance through the use of the five poles to signify importance. Look at verse two:

> *2 So Jacob said to his family and all who were with him, "Get rid of the foreign gods that are among you. Purify yourselves and change your clothes.*

Here is Jacob, the back slider, who when God says go, he said no and had runaway to this foreign land to get away from his sin and he had allowed his life to slide further and further away for God.

> I remember the story about a farmer and his wife who were driving to town in their pickup truck. The farmer was sitting behind the wheel in silence. His wife was sitting over against the door, as far from her husband as she could get. After several miles she said, "You know, when we were first married we didn't sit this far apart." Her husband simply replied, "I ain't the one that moved." If you are not as close to God as you once were, guess who moved.

Many a church revitalizer when the going seems hard, fold to the pressure and slide away from the Lord when they should be bowing before the Lord and seeking His blessings and deliverance. Can you see Jacob? He has changed a lot. Fortune has smiled on his face and now he is financially wealthy. He has more cattle, more goats, more

159

camels, more grazing land, more property, more wealth than even his uncle Laban has.

Physically, he has grown into middle age from that young teenager of the previous passages. No longer the bronze tanned physique of the attractive shepherd boy. No longer the one who takes care of the sheep and the goats. He now has some others to take care of that for him. He is now living in the softness of success. He is not as strong as he once was. His eye sight is not as keen as in days gone by.

Certainly Jacob has changed financially and physically. But perhaps the biggest change is that he has changed spiritually. In Shechem he lost the presence and the power of God in his life. He is living in that country without favor and fellowship with God. He has lost the presence and the power of God in his life. He was converted a long time ago in Bethel. But not only is he a long way away from Bethel geographically, he is a long way from there spiritually. He has become a backslider from his conversion and while he thinks he is rich and has a life of abundance monetarily, he has become most poor spiritually.

Every Church Revitalizer would do well to remember the days of our salvation and the blessings of God given to us the moment we came to know Christ Jesus as our Savior and Lord.

Jacob had allowed idols to creep into his household. Shechem was an easier place to live a life uncommitted to God and full of everyday idols distracting one from following the Lord. Does the description describing Jacob describe any of you today?

We have seen tremendous changes in these last fifteen years since we entered a new millennium. We have houses that our parents never dreamed anybody could live in. We have wealth, affluence, convenience, and abundance beyond our imagination. Change is all around us and yet, often it is the church which wants to avoid making the necessary changes which will help our church get growing again. I wonder if we, like Jacob, might say we too have changed spiritually. Perhaps not for the better. Do you remember when you would get excited about the work of the Lord? Remember when you wanted to teach Sunday Bible Study or lead a small group? Some of you within this dear church often say things such as: "we were once so close, once this church was the center of our lives, once the Lord our God was so real here!" But you like Jacob have just drifted away from God.

When God Says Go, But the Sinner Says No
When God Says Go, But the Back Slider Says No

3. When God Says Go, But the Suffering One Says No – vs. 4-5.

Notice verses four and five:

> *4 Then they gave Jacob all their foreign gods and their earrings, and Jacob hid them under the oak near Shechem. 5 When they set out, a terror from God came over the cities around them, and they did not pursue Jacob's sons.*

The removal of the strange gods was required if God was to be sincerely worshipped by Jacob and his household. The necessity of having no other gods, but Jehovah was afterwards instructed upon Israel as a nation.

The suffering that Jacob experienced comes in a report as he sits in his tent. The messenger reports that two of his sons, Simeon and Levi, have just committed a horrible crime. We know that the crime was that they slaughtered all of the men of the Hivites.[79] Here is the father, Jacob, broken hearted over his sons who have gone such a way. Here he is trying to get his thoughts around this in his tent when a second messenger comes and declares that he has news about Jacob's daughter Dinah. What he hears is what will break any father regarding his children. He hears that she has become the victim of the way of the world. Shechem who is the son of Hamor the Hivite has seized her and defiled her.

Do you see him? When God says go, but the suffering one says no. I can see Jacob in his tent crying out to the Lord. "Oh Lord, how could this happen?" I am reminded of the Bible verse: "What shall it profit a man, if he gains the whole world and loses his soul." He

---

[79] C.f. Genesis 34.

had been disobedient to God and yet, in a moment of great hurt he cries out to the Lord.

Some of you might be in that same place today. You are saying or have said, "What is it all worth anyway, if I lose the joy I had in Christ Jesus? What is it all worth anyway, if I lose the fellowship I once had in the church? What is it all worth anyway, if I lose the love I had in the family of God? What is it all worth anyway, if I lose the real values of life that go on and on and make life really worth living? What is it worth anyway?"

When God Says Go, But the Sinner Says No
When God Says Go, But the Back Slider Says No
When God Says Go, But the Suffering One Says No

4. When God Says Go, But the Resuscitated Says Go – vs. 6-15.

The Lord begins to stir in the heart of this wayward one. God had to drive him to his knees with all of the terrible things which had come into his life. Though the Lord does not want to use affliction to get our attention, sometimes it is affliction that will teach us something we cannot learn any other way. Sometimes God has to drive us to our knees, before He can get us to stand on our feet again in strength. Driven to his knees, Jacob cries out for forgiveness and then, he stands taller than he has ever stood in his life. Read verses 6-15 with me:

> *6 So Jacob and all who were with him came to Luz (that is, Bethel) in the land of Canaan. 7 Jacob built an altar there and called the place God of Bethel because it was there that God had revealed Himself to him when he was fleeing from his brother. 8 Deborah, the one who had nursed and raised Rebekah, died and was buried under the oak south of Bethel. So Jacob named it Oak of Weeping. 9 God appeared to Jacob again after he returned from Paddan-aram, and He blessed him. 10 God said to him: Your name is Jacob; you will no longer be named Jacob, but your name*

will be Israel. So He named him Israel. 11 God also said to him: I am God Almighty. Be fruitful and multiply. A nation, indeed an assembly of nations, will come from you, and kings will descend from you. 12 I will give to you the land that I gave to Abraham and Isaac. And I will give the land to your future descendants. 13 Then God withdrew from him at the place where He had spoken to him. 14 Jacob set up a marker at the place where He had spoken to him—a stone marker. He poured a drink offering on it and anointed it with oil. 15 Jacob named the place where God had spoken with him Bethel.

He calls his family and all of his servants in and tells them about his conversion. He tells them that he has not lived before them like he ought to have lived and he has not shown the love of God in his life like he should.

For the Church Revitalizer and for the local church this means that some of us have to clean up our houses. We have to clean up our social life, our business life, and our spiritual life. If we are going to revitalize this church and see it return to faithfulness in Christ Jesus, we have got to get the world out of our homes and our churches. We must remove the pagan gods and all of the other forms of paganism which are symbols of the way of the world and remove them from our lives. Back in verse four, he said to bury them.

He said to mount up and get going. He declared his desire to go back and make a new start. Something can really happen in a church when all of us rise up and say: "We are going back, back to God and back to the things the church should stand for. We are returning to our beginnings at Bethel so we can move forward."

When God Says Go, But the Sinner Says No
When God Says Go, But the Back Slider Says No
When God Says Go, But the Suffering One Says No
When God Says Go, But the Resuscitated Says Go

5. When God Says Go, But the Saved Says Go – Genesis 28:10-22.

I hasten to point out a night scene back on the hills of Samaria. Jacob is a young boy and this is the boy's first night away form home. It is a cloudy night with the skies full of deep threatening gloomy overcast. He is a young boy lonely and fearful. He does not even possess a tent to protect him from the elements and to sleep in. Jacob has only a few personal belongings thrown over his shoulder on a tied up cloth to make a sack. He makes his bed on the cruel hard ground and he finds a rock for his pillow. Sleep comes hard that night for there are sounds of the jackal in the distance and the clatter of the owls near by. He is fearful and his heart is despondent.

On the hill alone and crying out to the Lord our God. "Oh God, help me please. Why did I ever commit the things I did? I know I was wrong." He cries out in a spirit of repentance. He cries from a lonely heart. "Help me Lord, please help me." And do you know what happens? The Lord God always hears that kind of prayer for repentance and responds immediately.

Then we are told suddenly in a dream that a shaft of light broke out of the heavens and shined down upon Jacob and there appeared a ladder and angels ascended and descended. Here the Lord opens up His heart and His heaven to this young lad. He confirms to him:

"The covenant I made to Abraham your Grandfather and your father Isaac, I will make with you. I accept you and I will make you a son of mine. You will be part of this covenant of promise."

Here we see that Jacob responded:

"Oh, God, I will make my covenant to you. I will commit myself and my life to you from now on. I will give you a tithe of all that I have and you shall be my God and I shall be your servant.

That was the covenant, the experience that Jacob had. We call it a conversion experience. It is my prayer today that you have had such

164

an experience as well. Have you had a time where you have given over to Christ Jesus all of your sins in your life and acknowledged Him as Lord?

I remember as a thirteen year old the exact time and the exact place when the heavens opened and the ladder from heaven stretched down and the Lord my God became a reality to me. On June 16, 1972 I made a personal commitment to Him with all of my life as a young teenager. At the time I did not understand everything as much as I do now, yet I understood all that was required of me was the simple acceptance of Jesus Christ as my Lord and Savior. I felt that day in my heart, the warm feeling that I still feel today and that was that God had accepted me and given Himself to me and I was saved.

Could you pluck the cords of your memory today and bring back some chorus' of a time previously and a place when you asked the Lord to come into your life? God heard your prayer and answered your prayer, and you were saved. That was your Bethel!

The next morning the scripture declares that Jacob took the rock he had used as a pillow the night before and set it upright as a pillar. He declared:

"I will call this place Bethel, it is here that I found God."

Conclusion

Going back to Bethel is a story of belated obedience. Twenty years before he had built an altar on the spot where he enjoyed the vision of the ladder and the angels. Vows do not lose their mandatory character by lapse of years. Men may, but God never does forget the promises, which are made to him. So Jacob comes to the place and he gets off of his camel and starts rebuilding the altar that was in need of repair.

The name given twenty years previously to the place is renewed, Bethel in verse fifteen. Yet now there is a slight modification. In verse seven it was "El-Bethel" and now it is "Bethel" to connect with the altar just reestablished. Jacob rebuilt his altar and so must you today my friend. It is a personal thing. So he rebuilds the altar and he falls on his knees and prays.

In my mind here is something I think he would have prayed:

"Lord forgive me! It is no one's fault except for me.
Not my wives fault, nor my servants, nor my sons. It
is not Uncle Laban's fault. I took them into the things
of the godless world. It is not my father Issac' fault.
It was my fault. I have sinned. Forgive me please. I
make a new start right here and right now. I want to
make a new change within me and I promise I will
serve you for the rest of my life.

As he finishes his prayer he opens his eyes and sees his wife knelt
beside him. Behind him he hears his two boys Simeon and Levi. His
daughter Dinah is along side of him.

God heard Jacob's prayer and He let him come back so he could
start over again. Jacob served God from that point forward and
became a chosen vessel for the bloodline of the Messiah that would
come. This is our challenge and invitation today for all of us as a
church and for each one of us as individuals.

Do you need to come back to Bethel? Will you come back today?
If God is speaking to you to return unto the Lord, I invite you to come.

Chapter 14

Being on Mission Brings Life

John 3:16

"For God so loved the world that He gave His only begotten Son, that whoever believes in Him should not perish but have everlasting life." (John 3:16 NKJV)[80]

*G*od created the church to be a mission organization. There is no disputing that fact. Every aspect of the Gospel communicates this message. The first century church modeled a missions approach. The New Testament letters are all about being on mission. After its birth the church spread very quickly. Even the Roman government's demand that the church disperse was used by God to expand the outreach of the church. What the enemy meant for evil, God used for good.

Being on mission can bring new life to a church. Church Revitalization is about getting the church to see outside the stain glass windows into a world where people desperately need the message of Christ. I have preached in many churches through the years that have over the doors leading out this sign. "You are now entering your mission field." That is so true, but I wonder how many people

---

[80] Scripture quotations are taken from the New King James Version (Nashville, TN: Thomas Nelson, Inc., Publishers, 1979, 1980, 1982).

really get the message. It is easy to leave church, drive through our mission field, pull into the garage at home, let down the door and never think about the mission field that exists all around us. Then we head back to church the next Sunday to sing our songs, hear sermons and fellowship with people who are already part of God's family. Ed Stetzer says, "According to our research in *Transformational Church*, the healthiest churches are those who are actively seeking to understand and invest in their communities. Some churches have built a bubble around themselves as protection from the world." [81]

That is not the purpose of the church. A church that is not on mission is not being obedient to the God who created it. A church not on mission will ultimately plateau and then enter decline. Where new birth is not happening decline is a natural result. Why did the first century church experience exponential growth? It grew because it was unapologetically responding to the mandate Christ had given it, the mandate "to make disciples of people of all nations." This mandate has not changed in the two thousand plus years the church has been in existence. How we do church may have changed, but the mission is the same. Stetzer points out that being on mission is not about size, it is about engaging the lost community around the church. A church can be large and not engage the community, while a small church may be effectively engaging the community where it is located. I know a church in rural Georgia that is doing just that. The church is located approximately 7 or 8 miles from the nearest town. The church is at the end of a dirt road and is surrounded by farmland. Yet, this church is seeing people come to Christ. It has grown from 10 or 12 in attendance to over 60 in a little over a year. Why? Because the pastor is modeling what it means to engage the community. When he meets an individual he asks, "When you attend church where do you attend?" When the response is, "I don't attend," he gives the person a business card and says, "I am your pastor." Often the initial response is, "But I don't attend your church." He then says, "That doesn't matter. When you have a need of any kind I want you to call me. Here is my cell number. Please feel free to use it as you

---

[81] Ed Stetzer and Thom Rainer, *Transformation Church* (Nashville, TN: B&H Publishing Group, 2010).

have need." After the pastor began this it wasn't long before people started calling about a sickness in the family, or a personal struggle, or to simply ask questions about spiritual things. Then it wasn't long after that these individuals started showing up at the church. Many have now trusted Christ and are actively serving in this rural church that has made the commitment to engage its community.

What will motivate an individual or a church to be on mission? There are many places in Scripture we could look for that answer. But, I believe the greatest motivation is a verse that is very popular. For all of us who grew up in church it was probably the first verse we memorized. The verse is John 3:16. "For God so loved the world that He gave His only begotten Son, that whoever believes in Him should not perish but have everlasting life." This one verse summarizes the Bible. All eternity rests upon its truth. If the words of John will not motivate us to be on mission, I don't know what will motivate us.

We should be motivated by **the scope of His love.** "For God so loved the world..." Why is it imperative we be on mission? We must be on mission because of the vastness of God's love. David said in the Psalms, "Your mercy, O Lord, is in the heavens; Your faithfulness reaches to the clouds." The earth orbits the sun. The light of the sun traveling at the speed of light takes about eight minutes to reach the earth. We are just one solar system in the Milky Way. The Milky Way is so large that at the speed of light it would take 100,000 years to travel across it! God's love is greater than the Universe.

But let's bring it back to earth. The population of our planet now stands over 7 billion people. God loves each and every one of 7 billion people as if they are the only one He has to love. Can you fathom it? He loves the people around each church that exists. No matter the color of their skin, their history, their like or dislikes, or anything else; He simply loves them. There is no one God doesn't love! A person could shake his fist in the air and say, "God, I hate You." The only response from heaven would be, "but I love you."

We must love the people He loves. Our problem is, if we are not careful, we will only love the people who are just like us. I remember my first girlfriend. I was in Kindergarten. Yes, I know; young love, or so I thought at age five. I remember as we learned to write, deciding I would send her a note. I wrote with many misspelled words, I like you; do you like me? Check yes or no! Her response, No! My heart was broken, and my life was ruined, at least until recess. I responded to this pretty little girl, "I don't like you either." I probably stuck my tongue out at her as well. I was too devastated to remember. Unfortunately, that is often the response of the church to people who do not immediately like us or attend our meetings. Maybe we don't come right out and say, "We don't like you," but we demonstrate it by ignoring them. We walk right past them without engaging them in conversation or friendship.

That is so unlike Jesus. Not only does John 3:16 tells us we are loved, Jesus demonstrated it in the way He treated people. He was drawn to people others, including very religious people, shunned. Look at Zacchaeus. Luke tells us Zaccheaus was a tax collector. He was commissioned by the Romans to collect funds for the Government. The Roman system encouraged corruption. Zacchaeus was no different than most of the people who worked for the Roman Government. He was dishonest. He was also curious about this person named Jesus. Due to not being a tall man he climbed into a tree to watch Jesus pass by. How shocked he must have been when Jesus looked up into the tree and addressed him. He must have been really shocked when Jesus told him he was going to his house to share a meal. Zacchaeus knew how the Jewish leaders felt about him, but here was a Jewish man desiring to spend time at his house. This encounter led to a changed man and a new disciple of Christ. He, whom the religious establishment disdained, Jesus demonstrated love to, and, as a result, brought him in to God's family. Jesus concluded his conversation with this transformed man by telling people this is the very purpose for which He came into the world. Luke 19:1-10.

We must take seriously "For God so loved the world…" The love of God compels us to be on mission. It compels us to lay aside every argument, every distraction, and every resistance in order to show people God's love.

We must be motivated by **the supremacy of His love.** "That He gave His only begotten son…" Being on mission is all about Jesus. Jesus is the one universal need in the world. God loved enough to send Jesus to die for the sins for the world. No one else has done that. I can't imagine giving up one of my children for anyone, but

God gave His son for everyone. Look at John 3:17, "For God did not send His Son into the world to condemn the world, but that the world through Him might be saved."

The cross must be more than church decoration or casual acknowledgment by the congregation. It must be central to all we do. Unfortunately the cross often gets lost as the central focus. In most cases, this is not intentional. It is the result of wrong priorities. Other things take center stage. Evaluate the activity of a church and it will quickly become obvious where the cross fits into the ministry. If the cross is about God loving the world to the point He gave Jesus to die for the sins of the world, then delivery of that message must be the number one priority! Mind you, it is not enough to just verbalize that truth in song and sermon. It must be embodied in the practice of the church. If Jesus' death for the world is really what it is all about then it must be more important than the continuation of programs that have long lost their effectiveness. It must be more important than me getting my way. It must be reflected in the budget, the ministries, and the attitude of the church. I periodically hear people complain because it is their understanding a particular church has removed the physical emblems of the cross from the Sanctuary. I certainly am in favor of the presence of the emblem of the cross. This was true in where I served as pastor. The cross was given a prominent place over the baptistery. I am more concerned that the truth of the cross permeates our ministry and motivates us to be the church 24/7 not just on Sunday when we are meeting. If Christ really died for the world, which He did, then the church must be willing to die to anything that stands in the way of taking this message to the world. Paul said it well. "I have been crucified with Christ; it is no longer I who live, but Christ lives in me; and the life which I now live in the flesh I live by faith in the Son of God, who loved me and gave Himself for me" (Galatians 3:20).

Why would we not be on mission when we have the "supreme love of God" to share with the world? How can we be content to do church as usual when we understand the meaning and scope of Jesus' death?

We must also be motivated by **the sincerity of His love.** "That whoever believes in Him should not perish but have everlasting life," is all about the need of man and God's response to that need. God is so sincere in His love; He gives eternal life to all who repent of their sin and place their faith in His Son. If every church could only grasp this truth I believe we would see a major turnaround in the 80% of churches that are plateaued or in decline.

What these words tell me is, one hundred years from today, all that will really matter is what a person did with Christ. It also tells me that the mission of the church is extremely important. We have good news in a world accustomed to bad news. That is the essence of the meaning of the word "gospel." It is good news! Often the meaning conveyed is "to announce good news." Now "announcement" is a word we understand in most churches. I remember when I first entered the pastorate and began preaching on a regular basis. Each week I was inundated with announcements. People would be handing me announcements to make as I headed up onto the platform. Everything from dinners, programs, meetings, birth announcements were given to me. In fact I remember one Sunday, in particular, when my wife even got in on the announcement marathon. As I headed into the pulpit she handed me a folded piece of paper as she whispered in my ear, "Open this and read it to the congregation." Needless to say, I was a little perturbed, but too smart to show it. She knew how I felt about announcements. During the "announcement" time I began to read off the things that were so important to certain people. I finally arrived at the folded piece of paper my wife had handed me. Agitation quickly turned to physical weakness as I read these words, "Larry and I are pleased to announce we are going to be parents again in a few months. That is how I learned we were having our second child. I kid you not. The church cracked up laughing and applauding. It was great!

Seriously though, we do have a very important announcement to make to the world beginning right at the church and extending to the nations. It is very good news. It is the best news a person can ever receive. Jesus tells us very clearly in Acts 1:8 "But you shall receive power when the Holy Spirit has come upon you; and you shall be witnesses to Me in Jerusalem, and in all Judea and Samaria, and to the end of the earth." What are we witnesses to as the church? We are witnesses to the Gospel, to the good news.

One of my favorite Scriptures is found in Acts 16. In this passage Paul and Silas are at Troas. In the night Paul has a vision of a man speaking to him. Look at verses 9-10. "And a vision appeared to Paul in the night. A man of Macedonia stood and pleaded with him, saying, 'Come over to Macedonia and help us.' Now after he had seen the vision, immediately we sought to go to Macedonia, concluding that the Lord had called us to preach the gospel to them." Oh that the church would hear the Macedonian call today and respond to it. "Macedonia" may be the neighborhoods within two or three blocks of the church.

Being on mission locally should lead the church to being on mission globally. When it comes to sharing the good news, it is not one or the other, it is both. We should as Jesus commanded, "go into all the world…" How can we send missionaries to the nations while we are not missionaries to the community where we live? At the same time, how can we ignore the call to be on mission in the state where we live, nationally and internationally? A church in balance is a church that has a well rounded view of missions.

John 3:16 compels us. We must not ignore the scope, supremacy, or sincerity of God's love. We must announce to the world, "God loves you enough to send a Savior who will give to you eternal life."

Chapter 15

The Seven Churches
of Asia Minor Sermon

Revelation 1:17-3:22

*17 When I saw Him, I fell at His feet like a dead man.
He laid His right hand on me and said, "Don't be
afraid! I am the First and the Last, 18 and the Living
One. I was dead, but look—I am alive forever and
ever, and I hold the keys of death and Hades. 19
Therefore write what you have seen, what is, and what
will take place after this. 20 The secret of the seven
stars you saw in My right hand and of the seven gold
lampstands is this: The seven stars are the angels of
the seven churches, and the seven lampstands are the
seven churches.*[82]

These seven letters to seven literal churches around Asia
Minor provide a laser focus of the spiritual condition in these
churches. John the Apostle and writer of the Book of Revelation was
no doubt a pastor and the Lord allowed him to compose these letters from his pastor's heart. He knew these churches and was able to

---

[82] The Holy Bible: Holman Christian Standard Version. (Nashville: Holman Bible
Publishers, 2009), Revelation 1:17–20.

display strengths and weaknesses for these local centers of worship. Each one of these seven messages is for every church in every century throughout this church age. Though we do not have time to consider in depth each verse in every section, it is important to consider these churches and the impact they provide for the field of church revitalization and renewal.

In Revelation chapters two and three, speak of local church revitalization with perhaps a clearer voice than any other passages within the New Testament. The seven Asian churches were real, historical, first century churches, yet the messages given to them are as relevant to the church worldwide. The letters are more in the nature of messages than letters. Each of the seven messages originates with an individual depiction of the Lord Jesus taken from the vision of Christ given in the first chapter of Revelation. Kendell Easley in the Holman New Testament Commentary says:

> Each one is a permanent reminder of the special relationship the risen Lord had with a congregation he loved. When Paul, Peter, John, James, and Jude wrote their epistles, they generally followed the customary five-point formula of the first century: (1) author and recipient names; (2) formal greeting; (3) prayer; (4) main message; and (5) formal conclusion. Jesus created a letter-writing formula found nowhere else: (1) a *characteristic* of the sender; (2) a *compliment* to the recipients; (3) a *criticism* against the recipients; (4) a *command* to the recipients; and (5) a *commitment* to all who overcome.[83]

It is an extremely arduous task to examine and assess a local church. Only Jesus can really do that perfectly. A church may appear to be one thing, and beneath the surface be something quite different! The Lord sees all of the good things and the not so good things on the inside. It is easy to be deceived at times with just the externals of a

---

[83] Kendell H. Easley, *Revelation*, Holman New Testament Commentary, vol. 12, Holman Reference (Nashville: Broadman and Holman, 1998), 33-36.

church. People smile and they are polite and you might leave saying they have it all together and it is going on at the church. I encourage you not to just search for a church that can meet all of your needs, but find one where your gifts can be utilized for the work of the ministry.

Let's look at the seven churches and see what they can teach us today regarding the need to consider embracing a long-term strategy for revitalization and renewal.

The Ephesus Church: Where the World Came to the Careless Church – 2:1-7.

> *"Write to the angel of the church in Ephesus: "The One who holds the seven stars in His right hand and who walks among the seven gold lampstands says: 2 I know your works, your labor, and your endurance, and that you cannot tolerate evil. You have tested those who call themselves apostles and are not, and you have found them to be liars. 3 You also possess endurance and have tolerated many things because of My name and have not grown weary. 4 But I have this against you: You have abandoned the love you had at first. 5 Remember then how far you have fallen; repent, and do the works you did at first. Otherwise, I will come to you and remove your lampstand from its place—unless you repent. 6 Yet you do have this: You hate the practices of the Nicolaitans, which I also hate.*[84]

Most churches, which begin falling towards a state of plateau or rapid decline begin by first becoming just a little off of center. They need to work towards realigning the focus and the goals of the church back towards the original goals once held by a growing and healthy church. Most churches, which find themselves in this place, do so due to carelessness of the rank and file. A once healthy church, which

---

[84] The Holy Bible: Holman Christian Standard Version. (Nashville: Holman Bible Publishers, 2009), Revelation 2:1–6.

began with a consuming passion for God, now finds itself becoming careless with the things of God and the world begins to creep in to all that it does.

The Lord Jesus knows the weaknesses of his churches as well as their strengths. Within this short message to the Church in Ephesus, He gives them both well-deserved compliments and well-defined challenges as to their shortcomings. The Ephesus Church had a history of great leaders with the Apostle Paul, Timothy, and later the Apostle John all serving as leaders within this church. Yet here is a church that has become proud and careless in its witness. They had forgotten that servants of the Lord as shepherds are, in fact, mere gifts given by the Lord God himself.[85]

A fundamental truth within church revitalization understands that church health, growth, and success are not guaranteed forever and that some churches need to be warned to worship Jesus and not the leader leading from the pulpit. Here is a church that had many good and great things happening, yet it became careless with its witness. It served others, was busy doing acts of kindness, labored exhaustively, endured various trials patiently, and sacrificed tremendously for the cause of Christ, yet even in the midst of its greatness it became careless. It forgot its "*first love.*" Even churches that appear on the outside as almost perfect, on the inside can become unfocused and drift into careless habits that hinder the gospel's advancement. With all of the successes and victories the church in Ephesus enjoyed, it was in danger of watching its light be extinguished. Read Ephesians and you will hear Paul speak of their love for Christ twenty times!

A church in need of Revitalization is described as one where: there is the plateauing or declining after a phase of recent or initial expansion; then the church experiences the beginning of a high turn-over of lay leaders; there becomes a shorter duration of stay of fully assimilated people within the work; the church morale and momentum level drops; the church coasts for a brief time and then drops again, only to see the cycle of decline repeated again and again. The result is the church hits a new low! This new normal is the first sign of a church in need. Sadly the Ephesian Christians were not

---

[85] C.f. Ephesians 4:11.

attentive in witnessing to the same faith in the outside world. This is what is meant when Christ reproves them for having left their *"first love."* The point is not primarily that they had lost their love for one another, nor is the point simply that they had lost their love for Christ universally. The idea is that they no longer communicated their previous passionate love for Jesus Christ by witnessing to Him throughout their world.

A church that loses its *"first love,"* is a church in danger, like the Ephesus church, of becoming a careless church and in need of revitalization. When we lose our diligence in our gospel witness we become careless, our spiritual gifts are depressed and therefore the chastisement by the Father is necessary.

The Smyrna Church: Receives the Crown of Life–2:8-11.

> *8 "Write to the angel of the church in Smyrna: "The First and the Last, the One who was dead and came to life, says: 9 I know your affliction and poverty, yet you are rich. I know the slander of those who say they are Jews and are not, but are a synagogue of Satan. 10 Don't be afraid of what you are about to suffer. Look, the devil is about to throw some of you into prison to test you, and you will have affliction for 10 days. Be faithful until death, and I will give you the crown of life. 11 "Anyone who has an ear should listen to what the Spirit says to the churches. The victor will never be harmed by the second death.*[86]

Often a church is quite healthy and just needs to keep on keeping on. This church at Smyrna was faced with many challenges, and yet it kept keeping on. This is a persecuted church. When a church continually faces such challenges it is often time to begin a re-visioning process within the congregation.

---

[86] The Holy Bible: Holman Christian Standard Version. (Nashville: Holman Bible Publishers, 2009), Revelation 2:8–11.

Have you ever seen a church that once was alive and vital begin to lose its focus and drive for the cause of Christ? That is a church that needs to work on its Re-visioning strategy! Any *Re-visioning* strategy works to help churches dream new dreams and accomplish new goals that lead towards re-growing a healthy church! This strategy is designed for a weekend retreat tailored fit to foster a sense of ownership and team ship related to discovering a shared vision for the church. Understanding the critical milestones necessary for a new vision will help foster healthy church practices that might have been lost. Something as simple as achieving a great goal of some sort can begin to launch a church back into a *Re-visioning* strategy. Something as simple and dangerous as the Lord's children taking an ill advised rest that resulted in a slowing or stalling of the momentum into a maintenance mentality can cause a church to become stuck.

Being faithful as individual believers as well as individual churches amidst persecution is found as a central truth in the second portion of Revelation Chapter two. Smyrna was a bitter place for the Christian believers as the large Jewish population bitterly opposed Christianity. When Domitian (AD 81-96) issued an edict declaring the worship of the emperor, suddenly all, except the Jewish population, were required to worship him all across the Roman Empire. Domitian exempted the Jews from this proclamation. The Jewish residents did not desire to see those Christians in Smyrna receive the same exemption and religious freedom. No words of indictment are given to the congregation in Smyrna! They may not have enjoyed the endorsement of men, but they certainly received the acclaim of God. The Lord did give them sincere words of admonition as they faced increased suffering: *"Do not be afraid."* The church at Smyrna was facing increasing persecution and spiritual warfare.

The name Smyrna means "myrrh" or "an offering of sacrifice." Smyrna is the church that suffered martyrdom for Christ and receives the crown of Life. It costs to be dedicated to Christ today and Smyrna was an example of such costs. The great truth regarding revitalization and renewal found within this portion of scripture is that as we endure persecution we are encouraged to continue being faithful understanding that while more oppression may come upon us as believers, our eternal inheritance is secured.

179

If you study church history you will see that during the second and third centuries there were ten great waves of persecution. These two Roman persecutions were from Emperor Nero to Diocletian. After the Neronian persecution, Christianity came under suspicion, since new religions were not acceptable in the empire. And Jews, who sometimes had no qualms in semi-revering other deities along with their God, often were only too willing to make the Roman authorities aware that the Christians were not a Jewish sect. This is a city that is still in existence today, the Turkish city of Izmir, which is in modern day Turkey. Even though there are few Christians today in Smyrna because Christians are persecuted today in modern Turkey, when our Lord Jesus Christ addressed His letter to the church at Smyrna, everything He has to say to them is praise. Our struggles are not with flesh and blood, but with the enemy, Satan, who uses people to achieve his purposes. The allegation is just, as those in Smyrna who claimed to be God's people, the Jews, proved by their actions that they were not worthy of the name, so those who claim to be God's people, the Christians, can prove by their actions to be the church of the living Lord.

If there is a key truth regarding church revitalization and renewal found in this section it is at the close of verse ten, *"be faithful, even to the point of death."* The persecuted Christians in Smyrna were not assured freedom from persecution. They were guaranteed something much greater, which was the grace to withstand the afflictions they faced without fear. They also received a pledge from the Almighty that, as the one who died and rose again to life, Christ would bring them through to receive the *"crown of life."* The Smyrna Christians were overcomers and they had nothing to fear. They would be escorted into glory wearing crowns.

The Church at Pergamum: Wedded to the World–2:12-17.

12 "Write to the angel of the church in Pergamum: "The One who has the sharp, double-edged sword says: 13 I know where you live—where Satan's throne is! And you are holding on to My name and did not deny your faith in Me, even in the days of Antipas,

180

My faithful witness who was killed among you, where Satan lives. 14 But I have a few things against you. You have some there who hold to the teaching of Balaam, who taught Balak to place a stumbling block in front of the Israelites: to eat meat sacrificed to idols and to commit sexual immorality. 15 In the same way, you also have those who hold to the teaching of the Nicolaitans. 16 Therefore repent! Otherwise, I will come to you quickly and fight against them with the sword of My mouth. 17 "Anyone who has an ear should listen to what the Spirit says to the churches. I will give the victor some of the hidden manna. I will also give him a white stone, and on the stone a new name is inscribed that no one knows except the one who receives it.[87]

The Church at Pergamum did not fair as well as the previous two churches. It was a compromising church that was wedded to the world. When working towards church revitalization and renewal these types of churches must begin refocusing themselves back on the Word of God and the deeper things of God. Conceding to the devil is very dangerous for the Christian church. The church at Pergamum was not only one that was wedded to the world and made concession after concession; it was a church that compromised its core beliefs in order to get along with the world. It was the leading religious center of Asia Minor.

Pergamum had the first temple dedicated to Caesar and promoted the imperial cult. In Revelation 2:13, it is given the name *"Satan's seat"* as a reference to how bad it was for true believers to live there. It was even worse for Christians in Pergamum than for those living in Smyrna. A believer and *"faithful witness"* named Antipas, was killed for refusing to go the ways of the world as so many were doing. In spite of intense suffering by the Christian church in Pergamum those believers were not without fault in God's eyes.

---

[87] The Holy Bible: Holman Christian Standard Version. (Nashville: Holman Bible Publishers, 2009), Revelation 2:12–17.

Today, this city is called Bergama and it is only 15 miles from the sea. At one time there was a vast library of at least two hundred thousand volumes at Pergamum. This library was at the time the second largest in the world. Marc Antony gave this library to his girlfriend Cleopatra and had it moved to Alexandria Egypt.

Within the church at Pergamum there existed a group of individuals who began compromising with the ways of the world and Christ says that he has something against them in that he hated their everyday practices and doctrines. In such an atmosphere as Pergamum it would be difficult for believers to maintain the high standard of their faith without running into the political and cultic conflict that was all around them. In this passage, God calls them teachers of the *"doctrine of Balaam"* (2:14) and said that they *"lorded it over"* others and led them away from God's teachings and practices. Balaam was a prophet who prostituted his individual gifts so he could earn money from King Balak who had hired him to curse the Israelites.[88] The Lord halted Balaam from cursing Israel and turned his curses into blessings.

The sad and revealing portion of this Old Testament story is that, by following Balaam's advice as Balak sought to make friends with the people of Israel, he led many to worship pagan gods and feast at their pagan altars. The visual compromise and example from the Old Testament served as an illustration of the church at Pergamum becoming wedded to worldly ways as it made compromises and concessions with the secular political world in which it lived.

The key truth in relation to church revitalization and renewal within this passage is that when a congregation or an individual compromises with the world in order to avoid or alleviate suffering, pain, or failure, they are committing spiritual adultery and being unfaithful to the Lord. Such a compromising, permissive spirit of idolatrous living is to be condemned. Churches cannot and must not harbor compromisers of the gospel. The image of the *"sword of my mouth"* is a warning to the church for not disciplining those compromisers who have entered the church fellowship. When church members

---

[88] C.f. Numbers 22–25.

argue wrongly that the church needs to have a closer alliance with the pagan culture they are never correct.

Repentance was called for and the only remedy for one's sin. "*Repent, therefore.*" Not only the Nicolaitanes, but the whole Church of Pergamos is called on to repent of not having hated the Nicolaitane teaching and practice.[89] Christ responds vehemently, to their compromise and declares that he will have none of it. The believers in Pergamum must repent, recognizing and forsaking their sins. The only cure Christ presents before this church is that they repent. In other words, Christ said they needed to have a change of mind. Christ gives the church no other option.

The Church at Thyatira: A Corrupted, Unrepentant, and Small Community Church–2:18-29.

> *18 "Write to the angel of the church in Thyatira: "The Son of God, the One whose eyes are like a fiery flame and whose feet are like fine bronze, says: 19 I know your works—your love, faithfulness, service, and endurance. Your last works are greater than the first. 20 But I have this against you: You tolerate the woman Jezebel, who calls herself a prophetess and teaches and deceives My slaves to commit sexual immorality and to eat meat sacrificed to idols. 21 I gave her time to repent, but she does not want to repent of her sexual immorality. 22 Look! I will throw her into a sickbed and those who commit adultery with her into great tribulation, unless they repent of her practices. 23 I will kill her children with the plague. Then all the churches will know that I am the One who examines minds and hearts, and I will give to each of you according to your works. 24 I say to the rest of you in Thyatira, who do not hold this teaching, who haven't known the deep things of Satan—as they say—I do not put any other burden on you. 25 But hold on to*

---

[89] Jamieson et al., Revelation 2:12-17.

what you have until I come. 26 The one who is victo-
rious and keeps My works to the end: I will give him
authority over the nations—27 and he will shepherd
them with an iron scepter; he will shatter them like
pottery—just as I have received this from My Father.
28 I will also give him the morning star. 29 "Anyone
who has an ear should listen to what the Spirit says
to the churches."[90]

The church at Thyatira was a corrupted, unrepentant, and small community church. It is an example of a church that needs to begin the work of renewal. Renewing a church, which has allowed the corruption of the world to creep in, is a challenge. Unless the rank and file of its membership will seek individual repentance, there can be no corporate repentance for the church to begin a fresh start.

Unlike many of the other cities mentioned in Revelation, only traces of the existence of the city of Thyatira remain today. It is interesting to note that the longest message to the seven churches of Asia Minor was sent to the smallest community. When one considers that this tiny community was the least consequential city of the entire group of Asian churches, the message delivered must be of such importance to the church of its day as well as the church of tomorrow that the relevance must not be missed. The spiritual battle that is waged within Thyatira is a strong parallel to the battle to be waged in the end times.[91] Jesus Christ is called within this passage *"The Son of God"* and it is the only time in the Book of Revelation that this phrase is utilized. John had to convey a message of severe warning and judgment to this congregation, which explains the description of the Lord as *"One whose eyes are like a fiery flame"* and *"whose feet are like fine bronze."*

The letter to Thyatira is the longest of the seven messages and stands as the centerpiece of the entire seven. It was some thirty miles southeast of Pergamum and was located on the Lycus River. It was

---

[90] The Holy Bible: Holman Christian Standard Version. (Nashville: Holman Bible Publishers, 2009), Revelation 2:18–29.

[91] C.f. Revelation 14-18.

a busy church within this city. Thyatiraians were very busy carrying out sacrificial ministry for the sake of others. Additionally, their works were growing and characterized by faith, love, and patience; so the church at Thyatira was not guilty of mere religious activity. The *"works"* for which this church is first recognized are not mere general deeds of Christian "service," but are works of persevering witness to the outside world. The Lord encourages the church at Thyatira to witness to the outside world.

Yet the church was not all blessings and benevolence, there was corruption and an un-repentant spirit within the church. The Lord found much to uncover and censure in the Christian assembly at Thyatira. No amount of loving and sacrificial works can compensate for lenience of evil. The church was sanctioning a false prophetess to sway the membership and lead them into compromise. *"You tolerate the woman Jezebel"* was declared. It is not very likely that this woman was actually called *"Jezebel,"* since such an infamous name would not be given to a child at birth. The name is symbolic: Jezebel was the idolatrous queen who enticed Israel to add Baal worship to their religious ceremonies.[92]

It is thought provoking to compare the churches at Ephesus and Thyatira. The Ephesian church was weakening in its love, yet faithful to judge false teachers, while the people in the church at Thyatira were growing in their love, but too tolerant of false doctrine. Both extremes must be shunned within the church.

Not only was the church at Thyatira accepting of evil, it was unashamed and unwilling to repent. The Lord allowed the false prophetess time to repent; yet she rejected the opportunity. The Lord then allowed her followers opportunity to repent; yet they also rejected the opportunity. His eyes of fire had searched out their thoughts and motives, and He would make no mistake. It is further revealing that the Lord threatened to use the entire church of Thyatira as a grave illustration to *"all the churches"* not to allow evil to infiltrate one's church. Jezebel and her spiritual children who had committed themselves to her false teaching would be sentenced to tribulation and

---

[92] C.f. 1 Kings 16–19.

death. God would judge the false prophetess and her followers once and for all.

But notice here that not everyone in the congregation was unfaithful to the Lord and, as such, the Lord had a special word for them. They had detached themselves from the false doctrine and compromising practices of Jezebel and her followers. Without much hoopla the Lord simply challenges them to *"hold fast to what you have"* and resist the evil *"till I come."*[93] The compromising people in Thyatira were following *"the deep things of Satan,"* which would lead to darkness and death. The Lord's overcomers would share the *"Morning Star."*[94] How heartbreaking it is when a local church progressively leaves behind the faith and loses its witness for Christ. It is not just the lost who need to repent, but also disobedient believers. If we do not repent and deal with the sin in our lives and in our churches, the Lord may judge us and remove our lampstand.[95]

The Church at Sardis: The Has-Been Dying Church – 3:1-6.

> *3 "Write to the angel of the church in Sardis: "The One who has the seven spirits of God and the seven stars says: I know your works; you have a reputation for being alive, but you are dead. 2 Be alert and strengthen what remains, which is about to die, for I have not found your works complete before My God. 3 Remember, therefore, what you have received and heard; keep it, and repent. But if you are not alert, I will come like a thief, and you have no idea at what hour I will come against you. 4 But you have a few people in Sardis who have not defiled their clothes, and they will walk with Me in white, because they are worthy. 5 In the same way, the victor will be dressed in white clothes, and I will never erase his name from*

---

[93] C.f. Revelation 3:3; 16:15; 22:7, 17, 20.

[94] C.f. Revelation 22:16.

[95] C.f. Revelation 2:5.

the book of life but will acknowledge his name before My Father and before His angels.

6 "Anyone who has an ear should listen to what the Spirit says to the churches."[96]

The church at Sardis was the "has been" dying church. It is an example of a church that needs to utilize the restart strategy for church revitalization. It was a church crippled in its practices.

This is the hardest type of church to revitalize and often only happens once the church's patriarchs and matriarchs have tried everything else they can think of to grow the church with no success! The challenge here is that most churches wait too long to enter into this area of revitalization and by the time they are willing to utilize this strategy, they have sucked out all of the life within the church and it is no longer a viable candidate for this effort.

When a sick church no longer has the courage to work through the various issues that led to its poor health, it is usually identified as being on life support and in need of a restart. This type of church has been flat-lined and just holding on by means of its legacy and the faithful few who attend. The Restarting Strategy is for an unhealthy church to once again begin growing and to engage in a renewed vision that is demonstrated through sufficient evidences of hope. The restart based church revitalization model is being used all across North America. Being aware of their "critical" condition, however, is not enough. They have got to become convinced they need "major" surgical treatment. One church I have worked with still believes that they have more to offer, though their decline has been meteoritic and yet they refuse to allow a restart to take place.

Changing the mindset of the residual membership can often be very difficult. Senior adults occupy most of these restart candidate churches for which change is often hard to come by. Until the church is ready to make drastic changes, it is useless to become involved. There are thousands of churches like this all over America. One

---

[96] The Holy Bible: Holman Christian Standard Version. (Nashville: Holman Bible Publishers, 2009), Revelation 3:1–6.

startling phenomena is there are churches today that as the laity begin to depart this life often see nothing wrong with taking the church to the grave as well. That was never part of God's plan for the very thing He gave up His life.

Becoming comfortable within the church is an age-old problem that certainly was confronting the churches of Asia Minor. Compromise was becoming the order of the day and believers were being challenged to conform to the world rather that the Word of God. All the churches were facing the enticement to compromise and some of the churches such as Pergamum, Thyatira, Sardis, and Laodicea were surrendering to this enticement.

Sardis was alive in name only, the city, which in former times was vibrant and growing, now is a shadow of its former glory. As an example towards revitalization and renewal the church of Sardis is a warning that living on past glories will not suffice. The Lord criticizes the vast group of followers in the church for their spiritual stupor.

The former movement that was happening within the church towards growth now is headed towards becoming a stone relic and monument to the past. Hope was still available, but if it dragged its feet much longer, all hopes of revitalizing the church would be lost. The church at Sardis needed the life that only Jesus through the Holy Spirit could provide.[97] For the church living in past glories, seeking to muster up some form and function of previous programs, which were effective, does not always mean that new growth will result. When man is behind programs rather than the Lord, doom and lack of transforming life are more in effect. The "has been" church here was frail in its existence, feeble in its function, foolish in its approaches, and fruitless in its form. While there was still a tiny remnant within the church that was alive, most of the following was conforming to the world over commitment in the faith. In light of revitalization and renewal, there are times when a church is dying and it appears to be the pastor's fault, here there is no mention of removing the "*star*" and putting a new shepherd in place.

The Sardis church had no words of criticism and no words that challenged their doctrinal view. There was no mention of persecution

---

[97] C.f. Ephesians 4:4.

from the community to the church as in other instances within the seven churches of Asia Minor. A point can be made that, unlike some of the others that were indeed facing persecution, the church in Sardis had become so comfortable conforming to the pagan world they lived in that their comfort was because they had yielded to the ungodly culture around them. The has-been church had lived in the past for so long it no longer felt like it could make a difference. The evangelistic force and gospel witness it once had appears to be lacking as John writes his letter. Speaking to revitalization and renewal, most has-been churches, sometime in their journey towards decay, simply go to sleep and, if they wake up at all, they discover they are dead. The impression of the Church at Sardis is that the entire congregation lacked the aggressiveness necessary to continue its bold witness to the city. The gospel was not advancing in this church and was viewed by the community as neither needed nor evangelistically daring enough to reach them with the gospel. Their decaying witness was exemplified by their decaying impact on the community they were called to reach.

The Lord signals his concern when he declares, *"Be alert and strengthen what remains."* The guards are sleeping and one of the initial steps towards revitalization in a has-been church is a realistic assessment that things are not what they ought to be. *Dead* cells cannot produce those that are alive and reproducing. Some of the challenges for revitalization and renewal seen in the Sardis church were that they needed to repair the situation, restore their witness, replace comfort with evangelistic compassion for the lost, and begin to reproduce other followers of Christ.

Has-been churches lack the zeal to regain the charge and complete the task. These churches, such as Sardis, lack the faith to testify boldly and openly regarding Jesus. Those that do not are plateaued, dying, or already dead. Spiritual lethargy had seeped into the fellowship at Sardis and it is still a challenge for churches today.

God gives a brief formula for revitalization when he challenges them to *"be alert,"* remain *"watchful,"* *"repent,"* *"remember"* the Word of God, *"complete"* the task of God and do what it declares. The inspiration in this passage for revitalization is there is not a church that is beyond hope so long as a remnant remains that is willing to strengthen those that remain and reach others with the gospel.

The Church in Philadelphia: The Holding-on Faithfully Serving Church–3:7-13

> 7 *"Write to the angel of the church in Philadelphia:*
> *"The Holy One, the True One, the One who has the key*
> *of David, who opens and no one will close, and closes*
> *and no one opens says: 8 I know your works. Because*
> *you have limited strength, have kept My word, and*
> *have not denied My name, look, I have placed before*
> *you an open door that no one is able to close. 9 Take*
> *note! I will make those from the synagogue of Satan,*
> *who claim to be Jews and are not, but are lying—*
> *note this—I will make them come and bow down at*
> *your feet, and they will know that I have loved you.*
> *10 Because you have kept My command to endure,*
> *I will also keep you from the hour of testing that is*
> *going to come over the whole world to test those who*
> *live on the earth. 11 I am coming quickly. Hold on to*
> *what you have, so that no one takes your crown. 12*
> *The victor: I will make him a pillar in the sanctuary*
> *of My God, and he will never go out again. I will*
> *write on him the name of My God and the name of*
> *the city of My God—the new Jerusalem, which comes*
> *down out of heaven from My God—and My new name.*
> *13 "Anyone who has an ear should listen to what the*
> *Spirit says to the churches.*[98]

The church in Philadelphia was a church that was holding-on faithfully serving. These churches are often ones which need to reinvent themselves if they are to see new life once more. It was a consistent church which got locked in tradition and found itself faced

[98] The Holy Bible: Holman Christian Standard Version. (Nashville: Holman Bible Publishers, 2009), Revelation 3:7–13.

with a hard reality of not remaining viable to its changing community. Faithful churches are abundant today and God is to be praised. The church in Philadelphia was one that had a vision to reach a lost world and, as a result of this great vision, the Lord God set before them an *"open door that no one is able to close."* Their great love for a lost world and their desire to reach unbelievers with the gospel is why the Lord declares that no one will be able to close their door. Our New Testament speaks to an *"open door"* as an opportunity for doing the work of ministry.[99] It is interesting to note that the two places that Christ had no condemnation for are still in existence today. This is the one church besides Smyrna that Christ had no word of condemnation. There is a reason for that and it is because the people had turned to the Word of God.

The church at Philadelphia was given a wonderful opportunity for ministry. Philadelphia was situated in a strategic place on the main route of the Imperial Post from Rome to the East, and thus was called "the gateway to the East." It was located forty miles southeast of Sardis and, like the Sardis community, faced the long-term effects of the AD 17 earthquake, as did these community dwellers.

Attalus Philadelphus, who was the king of Pergamos, built Philadelphia. The city of Philadelphia is called the "city of brotherly love", and is named because of the love that Attalus II had for his brother, Eumenes, who was king of Pergamum.

Philadelphia sat on a geological fault and was destroyed by a severe earthquake that also destroyed Sardis and ten other cities. As a result the inhabitants planned for the event of future quakes. Nothing is known of the church at Philadelphia yet the Apostle Paul connected these inhabitants to his ministry in Ephesus. It was also called "little Athens" because of the many temples in the city. The church was certainly located in a place of tremendous opportunity.

Yet, in the midst of opportunity, there were challenges. At least two are found in this passage and are reminders of obstacles often faced in revitalization of churches. The first challenge was their lack of strength as seen in John's declaration *"Because you have limited*

---

[99] C.f. Acts 14:27; 1 Corinthians 16:9; 2 Corinthians 2:12; Colossians 4:3.

strength." The Lord provides the church in Philadelphia, which is weak, God's abundance of power to rely upon so the world might see and give God all of the glory and praise. A faithful church it seems, but with a small group of congregants. They were keeping God's Word as seen in the reference *"have kept My word"* and they were not afraid to bear witness of the Lord Jesus as John declares they *"have not denied my name."* When a church is faithful in the call of God and his commands, size really does not matter.

A second challenge and obstacle was found in the Jewish opposition in Philadelphia. The leaders of the Jewish synagogue excluded Jewish believers from worshiping in the synagogue. In the midst of the challenges, the Lord gives three declarations or promises to those of the church in Philadelphia. First, he says that he will take care of their enemies when he declares: *"I will make them come and bow down at your feet, and they will know that I loved you."* An emphasis for revitalization and principle would be that God will take care of our battles if we keep our lives focused on His work. Secondly, God will keep them from the tribulation. *"Because you have kept My command to endure, I will also keep you from the hour of testing that is going to come over the whole earth"* (v. 10). John then adds that the Lord *"will come quickly"* to finish this declaration. The final declaration and promise to the believers in the church of Philadelphia is *"I will make him a pillar in the sanctuary of My God, and he will never go out again."* God is going to honor their steadfastness and commitment to the gospel. The Lord desires for us to be faithful pillars and any church working towards revitalization and renewal needs a committed core of these types of individuals.

Part and parcel for the work of revitalization is the ability to realize if God opens a door ,we are to work aggressively while there is still time. If the Lord closes a door of opportunity, we must wait patiently. Both require faithfulness to see past the obstacles and seek the opportunities.[100] Preservation is a mark of church revitalizers and the church in Philadelphia, though small, had its share.

---

[100] C.f. 1 John 2:28.

Archeologically interesting is among the Seven Churches of Asia Minor that the church at Philadelphia still stands straight. One single column still is standing on site. Perhaps a pillar of honor representing a still open door towards evangelization and revitalization is Philadelphia proudly holding on and faithfully serving the Lord Jesus.

The Church in Laodicea: The Self-sufficient Apostate Church–3:14-22.

> *14 "Write to the angel of the church in Laodicea: "The Amen, the faithful and true Witness, the Originator of God's creation says: 15 I know your works, that you are neither cold nor hot. I wish that you were cold or hot. 16 So, because you are lukewarm, and neither hot nor cold, I am going to vomit you out of My mouth. 17 Because you say, 'I'm rich; I have become wealthy and need nothing,' and you don't know that you are wretched, pitiful, poor, blind, and naked, 18 I advise you to buy from Me gold refined in the fire so that you may be rich, white clothes so that you may be dressed and your shameful nakedness not be exposed, and ointment to spread on your eyes so that you may see. 19 As many as I love, I rebuke and discipline. So be committed and repent. 20 Listen! I stand at the door and knock. If anyone hears My voice and opens the door, I will come in to him and have dinner with him, and he with Me. 21 The victor: I will give him the right to sit with Me on My throne, just as I also won the victory and sat down with My Father on His throne.*
>
> *22 "Anyone who has an ear should listen to what the Spirit says to the churches." [101]*

---

[101] The Holy Bible: Holman Christian Standard Version. (Nashville: Holman Bible Publishers, 2009), Revelation 3:14–22.

The last church is the church in Laodicea: which was the self-sufficient apostate church. It is a cooled off lukewarm church which best opportunity for revitalization is restoration. Jesus is locked out of these type of churches due to their sense of superiority and self sufficiency. Arrogantly they believe their way is better than God's way.

Arrogance and a sense of self-sufficiency have been around for a long time. It is apparent in society and sadly into the local church. Wealth often gets in the way of serving the Lord Jesus. Laodicea was well known for its wealth and it had two specific industries, which brought it its wealth. It manufactured a distinctive eye balm for use in its flourishing medical center, as well as a glossy black wool cloth. Laodicea was located near Hierapolis, where there were famous hot springs, and Colossae, known for its pure, cold water. Hierapolis had hot medicinal waters; Colossae had cold, pure, refreshing water.

Located 43 miles southeast of Philadelphia[102] eleven miles west of Colossae, six miles south of Hierapolis,[103] and ninety miles east of Ephesus, it was an important trade center. Laodicea served as a gateway to Ephesus, which was the entryway to Syria.[104] Formerly it was known as Diospolis the city of Zeus. Around 250 BC Antiochus II, the ruler of Syria, further extended his influence to the west as he conquered the city and renamed it in honor of his wife Laodice.[105] As were the previous two churches located in the earthquake zone this city also lay in the regional path. Due to the earthquakes, Laodicea had to pipe in its water to the community. This was accomplished through a system of aqueducts, which feed the city. In seasons of drought it was vulnerable. In times of war, their enemies could disrupt the flow of water into the city.

In Colossians 1:7 we learn that Epaphras perhaps planted the church at Laodicea.[106] Churches were also planted in Hierapolis and

---

[102] Simon J. Kistemaker, *New Testament Commentary: Exposition of the Book of Revelation* (Grand Rapids: Baker Books, 2001), 166.

[103] C.f. Colossians 4:13.

[104] Kistemaker, NTCR, 166.

[105] Ibid.

[106] C.f. Acts 19:8-10; 20:31.

Colossae[107] during the Apostle Paul's three-year ministry in Ephesus. So foolish was the church that as the Lord was about to tell them the truth about their spiritual condition, they refused to believe His diagnosis. *"The Amen,[108] the faithful and true Witness"* the Lord declares. God speaks truth, is truth, and conveys truth because He is the faithful and true witness.

Jesus is the faithful witness and those believers in the Laodicean church were implicated for their ineffectiveness of faith. God does expect a level of competence as a believer and Christ follower. Was their witness nonexistent as so many are today,or was the finding of middle ground an offense to the Lord who desires our witness?

Often in the area of church revitalization, foolishness is accompanied by blindness to the real needs of the church and displays an unwillingness to face present realities. *"I know your works, that you are neither cold nor hot."* The church of Laodicea was without the stamina, strength, and staying power to spiritually press on for Christ. They had become worthless in their focus of self-sufficiency. *"I wish that you were cold or hot."* John declared that they have a lukewarm existence toward the Lord and it is repelling. The word *lukewarm (chliaros)* appears only here in the New Testament. The sense "unusable" or "barren" hits the mark. If the interpretation in the preceding paragraph is correct, Christ's threat to *spit you out of my mouth*—literally "vomit"—means that he will judge and reject them for their self-righteousness or self-sufficiency (rather than for their lack of spiritual fervor).

> A visual is in play here; the aqueducts usually delivered water to the city that was not cold and refreshing or warm and soothing. Members within this church were unaware of their need as they were more focused on their personal comfort, happy with complacency,

---

[107] As believers in Jesus Christ, we have every reason to be "fervent in spirit" (Rom. 12:11). Fervent prayer is also vital (Col. 4:12). This Epistle is thought to have been written to the Laodicean Church by Paul (Col 4:16). It was as the Emmaus disciples listened to the Word that their hearts were warmed. Paul had directed that the Christians in Laodicea read the letter to the Colossians.

[108] C.f. Isaiah 65:16.

and numb to the things around them. Feel the impact
of falling into a cold iced creek in the winter and one
would immediately feel the sensation. Put your feet
into a hot sauna and your senses would become alert,
but the Christians in Laodicea were anything but alert.

The church was self-regulating, self-satisfied, self-absorbed, and
self-sufficient. All of these are fatal dangers in a lukewarm church.
How often in church revitalization does there exist a difference of
analysis? This church thought like so many today, that it was in a
great situation only to find that the Lord had a different view. When
a church rests on its financial pedestal, it might just become blind in
its spiritual health, which is never indicated by an economic pedestal.

The particular "work" which is viewed as ineffective is that of
their efforts *to witness*. The unbelievers of the city were receiving
neither spiritual healing nor life because the church was not actively
fulfilling its role of witnessing to the gospel of Christ. Two reasons
suggest that the issue of witness was the specific concern:

(1) This is the issue for which all of the other churches
are either applauded or condemned, and it would be
unusual that the Laodicean situation would be different from the others;

(2) Christ introduces himself as the "faithful and true
witness," and since all of the self-descriptions of the
other letters are uniquely suited and related to the situations of the particular churches, the same is likely
the case here.

The foolishly self-absorbed church displayed that they had lost
their tenets and beliefs. While many looked upon themselves as rich,
in fact they were the most poor spiritually of all the seven churches.
When a church's beliefs and spiritual convictions are replaced by
pride, its ability to see its state in the Lord's eyes is blinded. *"I am
going to vomit you out of My mouth"* is God's declaration of the
nausea and revulsion they bring. *"You are wretched, pitiful, poor,*

blind and naked," he declares. When churches' beliefs are replaced by the perverted values of the business world, nausea will occur.

The Lord sketches three parallel pictures of the church's life:

First, the church said, I am rich, but Christ calls the Laodicean church poor.

Second, the church thought it was clothed with plenty of righteous character. Yet the Lord understood that it was spiritually wretched, pitiful, and naked.

Third, the church supposed itself to have spiritual insight. Instead it was blind. The city of Laodicea was famous for its medical school that exported a powder used for eye salve. Such medicine could not salve their blind eyes.

Even sadder than these three deficiencies is Christ's declaration that *you do not realize it.* This church had deceived itself about its spiritual condition. Reality was blinded by their personal agendas. *"Listen, I stand at the door and knock. If anyone hears My voice and opens the door, I will come in to him and have dinner with him."* The Lord Jesus is standing right outside, but the church at Laodicea just did not need him.

When a church gets so preoccupied with building its own little kingdom, the greater Kingdom with a heavenly concern for a dying lost world plays second fiddle to the self-absorption of the fickle and foolish. Their passivity led to their failure to press the message of Christ Jesus. They had no interest in giving witness and serving for the Lord. Advancement of the gospel in this congregation was lacking. *"I know your works,"* the Lord declares in an implication that there were none.

Finally the Church at Laodicea was *"naked"* in the eyes of God. Though the city was a place for wool manufacturing, these believers walked around fully clothed, and yet, they were uncovered and unprotected. In the Old Testament, nakedness meant to be defeated and humiliated.[109] Being clothed in an array of fine garments was not their real need. They needed to be clothed in the eternal forgiveness of Christ Jesus. God's grace and righteousness was in need. Notice in the passage that the Lord only offers the invitation to those few. *"If*

---

[109] C.f. 2 Samuel 10:4; Isaiah. 20:1-4.

anyone hears" was not an offer to everyone in the church of Laodicea. They were an independent church that had wanted for nothing, but they were not abiding in Christ and drawing their power from Him.

Even these concluding remarks speak of the basis for revitalization and renewal as an invitation to renewal, is offered to those believers who are already saved, but have drifted. Individual repentance as well as corporate repentance is necessary in church revitalization. Are we living today in the Laodicean age of the church? These seven churches are all around us today and if we want to begin then journey towards church health and renewal, we must face the issues within these churches that confront us.

Now for the last time in these letters we hear our Lord say, *"He that has an ear, let him hear what the Spirit says to the churches."* You see it is not what the churches say about themselves that matters. It is not what the world says that matters. What really matters is what the Spirit says to the churches. We are to receive truth from God and dispense it to the world. But we do not originate truth. We do not think up the things that we would like to believe and spread that abroad. We are responsible to hear what the Spirit says to the churches and then to pass that along, as we function as salt and light in the world.

Chapter 16

Eternity Compels Us!

Hebrews 9:27-28

> *"And as it is appointed for men to die once, but after this the judgment, so Christ was offered once to bear the sins of many. To those who eagerly wait for Him He will appear a second time, apart from sin, for salvation."* (Hebrews 9:27-28 NKJV)[110]

There is much talk in church circles about Revitalization. This is a needed topic when the most conservative estimates tell us that 80% of churches in America are plateaued or in decline. Why should there be concern over this? Well, for one thing it is true; that which is not growing, ultimately dies. The U.S. Census Bureau gives us some startling statistics. In the U.S. over 4,000 churches close their doors each year. From 1990 to 2000, the combined membership of all Protestant denominations in the U.S. declined by almost 5 million members (9.5 percent), while the U.S. population increased by 24 million (11 percent).[111] Churches will not stay on a plateau forever. If there is not a turn around they will eventually die.

Another reason is a church in decline or in a plateaued state does little to impact people who desperately need Christ. Why does the

---

[110] Scripture quotations are taken from the New King James Version (Nashville, TN: Thomas Nelson, Inc., Publishers, 1979, 1980, 1982).

[111] U.S. Census Bureau, http://www.census.gov.

church exist? It exists to take the Gospel to the world! Jesus was very clear in this. Not only did He tell us this was our purpose, He modeled it for us, "for the Son of Man has come to seek and to save that which was lost." (Luke 19:10) When we are not taking the Gospel to people who need it we are not being the church.

There is an even greater reason, eternity! The Bible is very clear this life is not all there is. Hebrews 9 states it very succinctly and very directly. "It is appointed unto man to die once, but after this the judgment..." Christ died because there is an eternity where people will live either with God or separated from God forever. Again Hebrews 9 says, "...so Christ was offered once to bear the sins of many." It is important that we help the church to understand this truth. We must understand the importance of laying aside preferences, traditions, power struggles, and anything else that stands in the way of us taking the Gospel to people the Bible calls 'lost', people God loves, Jesus died for, and for whom eternity is at stake. Until we understand what the Bible says will happen after a person dies, I don't believe there will be the urgency in the church to be the church Christ established us to be.

During World War II there was a U.S. bomber named the *Lady Be Good*. This bomber was part of the 376th Bombardment Group based in Libya. On its first combat mission it met tragedy when it crashed some 440 miles beyond its base while returning from the mission. The pilot reported his automatic direction finder was not working and requested the location of the base. The crew failed to see the flares that had been placed around the field to direct the bomber to a safe landing. The entire crew was lost in this tragic accident.

Like the bomber, *Lady Be Good*, millions of people are on a collision course with death, yet totally unaware of their destiny. We must alert people to eternity and the hope that lies in Christ.

What happens to you one minute into eternity? While there are lots of theories there is one reliable source, the Bible. What does the Bible tell us?

First the Bible tells us **death comes to all.** "It is once appointed unto man to die..." We must come to grips with our finiteness. George Bernard Shaw said, "The statistics on death are quite impressive, one out of one people die."[112] Ecclesiastes 3:2 "A time to be born, And a time to die; A time to plant, And a time to pluck what is planted;" Job 4:19 tells us "we live in houses of clay." Luke 12 gives the story of a man who was very industrious. He gave his life to acquiring more stuff. When he reached a time he thought he could retire he received a shocking announcement from God. He learned he was going to die and would not be able to enjoy any of the things he had gained in this life.

Most folks have a superman mentality. Somehow they are going to escape death, but the truth is death is universal. None of us will be able to escape.

The time of death is uncertain. The Bible says, "It is appointed unto man once to die," but it doesn't say when. James 4:13-14 "Come now, you who say, "Today or tomorrow we will go to such and such a city, spend a year there, buy and sell, and make a profit"; whereas you do not know what will happen tomorrow. For what is your life? It is even a vapor that appears for a little time and then vanishes away." This is part of "sting of death." Unfortunately as a pastor I have done funeral services for people of every age, from the youngest to the elderly. As chaplain with police and fire I have had the unfortunate responsibility to notify scores of people of the "untimely" deaths of their loved ones. This is never easy. There are no words that are sufficient. Grief is very real.

The Bible also teaches **death is a door, not the end.** "It is appointed unto man to once die, but after this..." The phrase "but after this" is very important. It points to a continuation not an end. Eyes close in death on this planet and open in eternity. The Bible is very clear on this subject. You have several stories that support this truth. One is the story of the rich man in hell. He was very much conscious. He could speak, he recognized individuals, and he could speak on eternity. Then there are the thieves who were crucified with Jesus. While one was very angry and critical, the other realized his need and sought forgiveness. Jesus said to this man, "...Assuredly, I

---

[112] Roy B. Zuck, *The Speaker's Quote Book: Over 5,000 Illustrations and Quotations for All Occasion, Revised and Expanded* (Grand Rapids, MI: Kregel Publications, 2009).

say to you, today you will be with Me in Paradise." You have a beautiful picture of life's continuation in Stephen. While being stoned to death for his faith in Christ and his boldness to witness for Christ, Stephen saw something incredible. He then gives an account of what he saw. "But he, being full of the Holy Spirit, gazed into heaven and saw the glory of God, and Jesus standing at the right hand of God, and said, "Look! I see the heavens opened and the Son of Man standing at the right hand of God" (Acts 7:55-56)!

This answers several popular theories. One theory is this life is it; nothing happens after death. Many believe we live and we die and that is the end of the story. Paul addressed this in a conversation on the Resurrection. In I Corinthians 15:19 he says, "If in this life only we have hope in Christ, we are of all men the most pitiable." It also answers the theory that the righteous do go to heaven, but the wicked just die. It also answers reincarnation. The Bible says, "...but after this the judgment," not appearance here on earth as a different person. There is a day we were born, but there will never be a day in the future when we do not exist.

Physical death leads to a meeting with God. "...the judgment." Every person meets God one day. Philippians 2: 9-10, "Therefore God also has highly exalted Him and given Him the name which is above every name, that at the name of Jesus every knee should bow, of those in heaven, and of those on earth, and of those under the earth, and that every tongue should confess that Jesus Christ is Lord, to the glory of God the Father." Death brings with it accountability. So often we hear people say, "I am accountable to no one." We all are accountable to God. Every knee will bow and every tongue will confess the Lordship of Christ either in this life or in judgment.

Two individual judgments are taught in the Scripture. There is the judgment of the unsaved. Revelation 20 talks about this judgment. "Then I saw a great white throne and Him who sat on it, from whose face the earth and the heaven fled away. And there was found no place for them. And I saw the dead, small and great, standing before God, and books were opened. And another book was opened, which is the Book of Life. And the dead were judged according to their works, by the things which were written in the books. The sea gave up the dead who were in it, and Death and Hades delivered up the dead who were in them. And they were judged, each one according to his works. Then Death and Hades were cast into the lake of fire. This is the second death. And anyone not found written in the Book of Life was cast into the lake of fire" (Revelation 20: 11-15). God has a book. The Book of Life contains the names of all who have trusted Christ as Savior. To reject Christ in this life is to face Him at the Judgment.

Then there is the judgment of the saved. The Bible calls this the Judgment Seat of Christ. "Therefore we make it our aim, whether present or absent, to be well pleasing to Him. For we must all appear before the judgment seat of Christ, that each one may receive the things *done* in the body, according to what he has done, whether good or bad. Knowing, therefore, the terror of the Lord, we persuade men; but we are well known to God, and I also trust are well known in your consciences" (2 Corinthians 5: 9-11). While the judgment of the lost is a place of regret; the judgment seat of Christ is a place of reward. Faithfulness is rewarded here.

After judgment there is eternity. The Bible teaches there are only two places in eternity. There is no middle ground and no replay. The Bible teaches that both heaven and hell are real. We don't hear much preaching on hell today. That may be in part to the fact there was a time that was the majority of preaching by some. While that is wrong, it is also wrong to try to ignore its reality. Jesus taught that hell is a real place. There are many references by Jesus in the Bible. "If your right eye causes you to sin, pluck it out and cast *it* from you; for it is more profitable for you that one of your members perish, than for your whole body to be cast into hell. And if your right hand causes you to sin, cut it off and cast *it* from you; for it is more profitable for you that one of your members perish, than for your whole body to be cast into hell" (Matthew 5:29-30). Again in Matthew 10:28 he says, "And do not fear those who kill the body, but cannot kill the soul. But rather fear Him who is able to destroy both soul and body in hell." Among other things hell is going to be a place of intense regret. The Bible says "there will be weeping and gnashing of teeth." When do we grit our teeth? When we realize we have made a huge mistake. I remember locking my keys in my car. As I closed the door I realized what I had done. It was too late. I grabbed for the handle but missed.

I grit my teeth and moaned under my breath, and that was over an event that was going to just cost me a little inconvenience and a little money. I believe there will be many people who will realize seconds into eternity the eternal mistake they made when they resisted Christ in this life.

The Bible also teaches there is a heaven. It, too, is a real place. My favorite passage on heaven is John 14:1-6. I have used it count-less times to comfort family members at the services of their loved ones who have died. "Let not your heart be troubled; you believe in God, believe also in Me. In My Father's house are many mansions; if *it were* not *so,* I would have told you. I go to prepare a place for you and if I go and prepare a place for you, I will come again and receive you to Myself; that where I am, *there* you may be also. And where I go you know, and the way you know. Thomas said to Him, 'Lord, we do not know where You are going, and how can we know the way?' Jesus said to him, 'I am the way, the truth, and the life. No one comes to the Father except through Me.'" (John 14:1-6) Heaven is a place prepared for all who will trust Christ. I believe when a Believer in Christ closes his eyes in this life he opens them in the presence of Christ. Paul said as much in his second letter to the church at Corinth. "So we are always confident, knowing that while we are at home in the body, we are absent from the Lord. For we walk by faith, not by sight. We are confident, yes, well pleased rather to be absent from the body and to be present with the Lord" (2 Corinthians 5: 6-8). Heaven is a place where there will be no more pain and suffering. I think we would all agree that there is much pain and much suffering in our world today. You only have to check any news outlet to see intense suffering. The church is filled with people who are suffering physically, emotionally, and relationally. I have good news. One day this will be alleviated. There will be no more pain. "And God will wipe away every tear from their eyes; there shall be no more death, nor sorrow, nor crying. There shall be no more pain, for the former things have passed away" (Revelation 21:4). I say amen to that.

We have walked through the process from death to eternity. How can we, the church, knowing these things, ignore the responsibility and opportunity to represent Christ the way we should in today's world? When we compare it to eternity do our preferences, attempts at power in the church, resistance to change really add up? What are we willing to do that the Gospel can be more effectively carried to the world? I pray we will gain an eternal perspective. The world is counting on us. Jesus is counting on us. I am going to make a statement that will initially meet with resistance. I know when I first heard it in a conference years ago I resisted it a little bit; that is until I thought it through. The statement is this. "The hope of the world is the church." Our immediate response is to say, "No, Jesus is the hope of the world." That is right, but let me take it a step further. Who did Jesus leave with the mandate "to make disciples of all people?" It wasn't the local civic organization and it wasn't the government. It was the church. So, in essence, if the world is going to hear the Gospel and respond to the Gospel, it will be because the church is faithful. If people are to spend eternity with Christ in heaven it will be because the church determines that is the priority and everything else falls in line behind that goal! We have to choose. We must choose right, because eternal matters are at stake.

Conclusion

evitalization is a process. It is one that takes time, commitment, prayer, and a willingness on the part of people to experience change that brings a new vision and passion to the church.

It is the prayer of Dr. Cheyney and myself that the collection of sermons found in this book will inspire you and assist you in the Revitalization journey. As you cover this material with prayer, infuse your personality and delivery style it is our desire God use these sermons to ignite a fire in the people of God that will lead to a renewed commitment to taking the Gospel to the world.

Our time is short. God has given each of us a window of opportunity to make an impact on the world. There is no greater mission than the mission given to the church. The impact the church has is eternal in nature. A church that catches the vision for Revitalization can have unlimited influence in a community. May God use you and hopefully, the inspiration you will receive from reading and applying these sermons, to have impact beyond your greatest dreams. We pray God's blessings on you as you seize the opportunity.

CPSIA information can be obtained at www.ICGtesting.com
Printed in the USA
LVOW06s1120081215

465930LV00001B/107/P